FOLK TALES FROM TIBET

FOLK TALES FROM TIBET

WITH ILLUSTRATIONS BY A TIBETAN ARTIST AND SOME VERSES FROM TIBETAN LOVE-SONGS

COLLECTED AND TRANSLATED

BY

CAPT. W. F. O'CONNOR, C.I.E.

Secretary and Interpreter of the Mission of Lhasa (1904)

GYAN

Published by

Gyan Publishing House
5, Ansari Road
Daryaganj, New Delhi-110002
Phone: 011-47034999, 9811692060
E-mail: books@gyanbooks.com

Distribution Network
gyanbooks.com
India, USA, Canada, UK, Australia, France

ISBN : 978-81-212-2896-1 (HB)
First Published, 1906

2nd Impression 2021

Printed at: Gyan Press, Delhi.

Folk tales From Tibet
Author: CAPT. W. F. O'Connor

FOLK TALES FROM TIBET

WITH ILLUSTRATIONS BY A TIBETAN ARTIST
AND SOME VERSES FROM TIBETAN
LOVE-SONGS

COLLECTED AND TRANSLATED

BY

CAPT. W. F. O'CONNOR, C.I.E.

Secretary and Interpreter of the Mission to Lhasa (1904)

LONDON
HURST AND BLACKETT, LTD.
182, HIGH HOLBORN, W.C.

1906

THE CHAPEL RIVER PRESS
KINGSTON SURREY

PREFACE.

In presenting these little stories to the public, it may perhaps be of interest if I describe how I came by them.

During two years spent in Tibet, at Gyantse, Lhasa, and elsewhere, I have made many friends amongst all classes of Tibetans—high and low, rich and poor—and have conversed with all sorts of persons upon all sorts of topics. In the course of my wanderings I learned that there exists amongst this fascinating and little-known people a wealth of folk-lore, hitherto inaccessible to the outside world, and I made efforts to collect as many of their stories as I could.

For certain special reasons this quest proved more difficult than I had anticipated. In the first place, I found that many of the best known stories had been imported bodily from India* or China, and possess but little of that local colouring which is one of the chief charms of folk-lore. Secondly, some of the very best and most characteristic stories are unfit for publication in such a book as this.† And, thirdly, human nature being much the same all the world over, it was not always

* Compare, for example, "Tibetan Tales derived from Indian Sources," translated from the Tibetan of the Kah Gyur into German by F. Anton von Schiefner. Done into English from the German by R. W. S. Ralston.

† But I am preserving such of these as appear to me to possess any scientific interest.

possible to find a suitable *raconteur* in a suitable mood for story-telling. A story told by a nervous or reluctant narrator loses half its charm. A good story must be natural, and necessitates sympathy on the part both of teller and of hearer. Armed diplomatic missions and an official position, apart from all questions of difference of language and nationality, do not tend to elicit the ideal sentiments necessary for the establishment of complete mutual confidence.

But patience, and the growth of kindly feelings on both sides, helped me to some extent to overcome the shyness and reluctance of the simple folk who have supplied me with my material; and, as time went on, I was able to coax a story from many unlikely sources. Village headmen, monks, servants, local government officials, peasants, traders—these and many others have contributed to my store. Shyly and haltingly at starting, with many bashful apologies and disclaimers, the story-teller will begin his tale. But a Tibetan audience is one of the best imaginable, and their open sympathy and appreciation soon melt the frosts of reserve, and the words flow freely. Presently all sense of constraint is lost, and I have known a story interrupted for ten minutes at a time by the uncontrollable merriment aroused by some comic incident.

Some of the stories, then, I have been obliged, reluctantly enough, to discard altogether for the present; others require further revision or elucidation. But the rest of my little store I give here, and with this one apology: that I have made no attempt to ornament or improve upon them. I have written them down just as I heard them, and have translated them, as accurately as I could, from the Tibetan idiom into ours. As to their origin or scientific bearing I say nothing, and put forward no theories. I leave the Tales to speak for themselves; but would invite, and shall cordially welcome, the criticisms and surmises of all students of folk-lore who are in a position to give an expert opinion upon such points, and to shed a light upon obscure corners into which I have been unable to penetrate.

I have added to the stories a few verses taken at random from popular Tibetan love-songs, as a sample of the wealth of imagery and genuine poetic sentiment which is to be found amongst the inhabitants of this strange country. Owing to the extremely idiomatic form and severe compression of Tibetan metrical compositions, the translation of these songs into anything even distantly resembling poetry, without altogether destroying the characteristics of the original, presents peculiar difficulties; and I must crave indulgence for their crudeness and lack of artistic finish.

The pictures are the maiden effort at book illustration of a Tibetan artist, resident at Gyantse, and are, I fear, somewhat weak in details, as owing to my absence from Gyantse during the time they were in progress I was unable personally to superintend their execution. For the excellent photograph which appears as the frontispiece I am indebted to my friend and companion at Gyantse, Capt. R. Steen, of the Indian Medical Service.

In conclusion, I must express my grateful acknowledgments to Mr. Perceval Landon, to whose suggestion the collection and publication of these Tales, as well as their illustration by a native artist, is in a great measure due; and I must thank him, moreover, for many valuable hints and much kindly sympathy and assistance.

W. F. O'Connor, Capt.

CONTENTS.

LIST OF ILLUSTRATIONS.

FOLK TALES FROM TIBET.

STORY No. I.

HOW THE HARE GOT HIS SPLIT LIP.

A HARE was going along a road one day, when suddenly, on turning a corner, he came upon a large Tiger. The Tiger at once seized the Hare, and said that he was going to eat him.

"Please, please, Uncle Tiger," said the Hare, holding up his thumbs in supplication, "please don't eat me, I am only a very small beast, and will make a very insufficient meal for a great big animal like you. And if you will spare my life I will take you to where you can find a much bigger, fatter creature than me for your supper."

"Very well," said the Tiger, "I agree to that. But if you don't show me a much bigger animal than you are, I shall certainly be obliged to eat you."

So he released the Hare, and the two walked off along the road together.

As they went along night began to fall, and when it was quite dark the Hare began smacking his chops and making sounds as if he was eating something very nice.

"What are you eating, Brother Hare?" asked the Tiger.

"I am eating my eye, Uncle Tiger," replied the Hare. "I have taken it out and eaten it; it is very nice, and it soon grows again."

The Tiger was rather surprised at hearing this, but being very hungry he proceeded to scrape out his own eye and eat it up. After going a little further the Hare again began smacking his lips, as if he was eating something.

"What are you eating now, Brother Hare?" asked the Tiger.

"I am eating my other eye, Uncle Tiger," replied the Hare; "it is even better than the first."

The foolish Tiger on hearing this proceeded to scrape out his other eye and eat that.

The Tiger was now quite blind, and the Hare led him along to the brink of a deep gulf, where he advised the Tiger to sit down and rest for a while. And after the Tiger was seated, the Hare said:

"Don't you find it cold, Uncle Tiger? shall I light you a fire?"

"Yes, please, Brother Hare," said the Tiger, "I think a fire would be very pleasant."

So the Hare lighted a fire just in front of the Tiger, and when it was blazing up he kept putting the sticks nearer and nearer the Tiger, so that the Tiger was obliged to keep edging further and further away, when all of a sudden he toppled over backwards into the gulf behind. Now it happened that half-way down the

THE HARE AND THE TIGER

gulf a tree was growing from a cleft in the precipice, and as he passed this the Tiger seized one of the boughs with his teeth, and so arrested his fall. The Hare, peeping over the edge, saw what had happened, and he called out:

"Oh, Uncle Tiger, Uncle Tiger, are you safe?"

The Tiger was afraid to open his mouth to reply, and all he could do was to growl, "M—m—m——"

"Oh, Uncle Tiger," said the Hare, "is that all you can say? I am afraid you must be very badly hurt. Do just say 'Ah!' and I shall know that you are all right."

The Tiger, anxious to please the Hare, opened his mouth to say "Ah!" and was instantly precipitated to the bottom of the gulf, where he fell upon some rocks and was killed.

Next morning the Hare went hopping down the road when he met a Man driving along a lot of Horses.

"Good morning, Father Man," said he to the driver. "Would you like to know where you can find a good Tiger's skin?"

"Yes, please, Brother Hare," said the Man, thinking he would sell the skin and make a lot of money.

So the Hare pointed out to him where the dead Tiger lay in the ravine, and the Man hastened off to skin it, after first asking the Hare to take care of his Horses while he was away.

As soon as he was out of sight the Hare saw two Ravens sitting in a tree overhead. He called out to them:

"Brothers Raven, look here! Here are a lot of Horses

with no one in charge. Why don't you come down and feed on the sores on their backs?"

The Ravens thought this was a good idea, and flying down, they perched on the Horses' backs, and began to dig their beaks into the sore places. The poor Horses, in fear and pain, soon stampeded, and galloped about all over the country.

The Hare then hopped on a little further down the road and came upon a Boy tending Sheep.

"Good-morning, Brother Boy," said the Hare, "would you like to know where there is a fine Raven's nest, full of eggs?"

"Yes, please, Brother Hare," said the Boy, thinking he would climb the tree and take the Raven's eggs. So the Hare pointed out to him the tree where the Raven's nest was, and the Boy ran off to get the eggs, after first asking the Hare to take charge of the Sheep for him while he was away.

The Hare soon espied a Wolf on the hill-side not far off, so he went up to him and said:

"Good-morning, Brother Wolf, do you know that there is a fine flock of Sheep quite unguarded down there, and I should advise you to take advantage of this opportunity of killing some of them."

The Wolf at once rushed down the hill into the middle of the flock of Sheep, scattering them all in every direction, and killing as many as he thought he required for his own use.

Meanwhile the Hare proceeded to the top of a high hill whence he could survey the whole country. From there he was able to discern the dead Tiger lying in the ravine, with the Man stripping off its skin ; the Horses careering all over the country, with the Ravens pecking at the sores on their backs ; the Boy robbing the Raven's nest ; and the Sheep, pursued by the Wolf, scattered to the four quarters of the compass.

The sight so amused the Hare that he leaned back on a handy stone, and laughed to such an extent that he actually split his upper lip. And it has remained split to this very day.

STORY No. II.

THE STORY OF THE TIGER AND THE MAN.

ONCE upon a time there were two Tigers who lived in a certain forest and had a family of three children. The Father Tiger grew old and began to fail, and just before his death he sent for his three children and addressed them as follows:

"Remember, my children," said he, "that the Tiger is Lord of the jungle; he roams about at his will and makes a prey of the other animals as he wishes, and none can gainsay him. But there is one animal against whom you must be on your guard. He alone is more powerful and cunning than the Tiger. That animal is Man, and I warn you solemnly before I die to beware of Man, and on no account to try to hunt or to kill him."

So saying, the old Tiger turned on his side and died.

The three young Tigers listened respectfully to the words of their dying parent and promised to obey; and the elder brothers, who were obedient sons, were careful to follow his advice. They confined their attentions to the slaughter of deer, pigs, and other denizens of the forest, and were careful, whenever they came within sight or scent of any human being, to clear off as fast as they could from so dangerous a neighbourhood. But the youngest Tiger was of an independent and inquisitive disposition. As he grew older and stronger he began to chafe against the restriction that had been imposed upon him.

"What, after all," thought he to himself, "can be this creature Man that I should not slay him if I wish. I am told that he is but a defenceless creature, that his strength cannot be compared to mine, and that his claws and teeth are quite contemptible. I can pull down the largest stag or tackle the fiercest boar with impunity. Why, then, should not I be able to kill and eat Man also?"

So after a while, in his conceit and folly, he determined to quit his own part of the forest and to venture forth towards the open country in search of a Man as his prey. His two brothers and his mother tried to reason with him and to persuade him to remember the words of his dying father, but with no avail; and finally, one fine morning, in spite of their prayers and entreaties, he set off alone on his search.

He had not proceeded very far when he met an old, worn-out pack-Bullock, thin and emaciated, and with the marks of many ancient scars on his back. The young Tiger had never seen a Bullock before, and he regarded the creature with some curiosity. Walking up to it he said:

"What sort of animal are you, pray? Are you a Man by any chance?"

"No, indeed," replied the creature; "I am only a poor Bullock."

"Ah!" said the Tiger. "Well, perhaps you can tell me what sort of an animal Man is, for I am just going out to find and kill one."

"Beware of Man, young Tiger," replied the Bullock; "he is a dangerous and a faithless creature. Just look at me for example. From the time when I was very young I was Man's servant. I carried loads for him on my back, as you may see by these scars, and for many years I slaved for him faithfully and well. While I was young and strong he cared for me and valued me highly; but as soon as I became old and weak, and was no longer able to do his work, he turned me out into this wild jungle to seek my food as best I might, and gave no thought for me in my old age. I warn you solemnly to leave him alone and not to try and kill him. He is very cunning and dangerous."

But the young Tiger only laughed at the warning and went on his way. Soon afterwards he came across an ancient Elephant wandering by itself on the outskirts of the forest, and feeding with its trunk on the grasses and foliage which it loves. The old animal had a wrinkled skin and a small and bleary eye, and behind its huge ears were many cuts and ancient scars, showing where the goad had been so frequently applied.

The young Tiger eyed this strange animal with some surprise, and going up to it he said:

"What sort of an animal are you, please? You are not a Man, I suppose?"

"No, indeed," replied the Elephant; "I am only a poor old worn-out Elephant."

"Is that so?" answered the Tiger. "Perhaps you can tell me, however, what sort of a creature Man is, as I am now hunting for one in order to kill and eat him."

"Beware how you hunt Man, young Tiger," replied the old Elephant; "he is a faithless and dangerous animal. Look at my case. Although I am the Lord of the jungle, Man tamed me, and trained me, and made me his servant for many years. He put a saddle on my back and made stirrups of my ears, and he used to strike me over my head with an iron goad. While I was young and strong he valued me highly. Food was brought to me, as much as I could eat every day, and I had a special attendant who used to wash and groom me, and to see to all my wants. But when I became old and too infirm for further work, he turned me out into the jungle to fend for myself as best I could. If you will take my advice you will leave Man alone, or it will be the worse for you in the end."

But the young Tiger laughed contemptuously and went on his way. After proceeding for some little distance he heard the sound of some one chopping wood, and creeping near he saw that it was a Woodcutter engaged in felling a tree. After watching him for some time the Tiger emerged from the jungle, and going up to the Man, he asked what sort of an animal he was. The Woodcutter replied:

"Why, what an ignorant Tiger you are; can't you see that I am a Man?"

"Oh, are you," replied the Tiger, "what a piece of

luck for me. I was just looking for a Man in order to kill and eat him, and you will do nicely."

On hearing this the Woodcutter began to laugh. "Kill and eat *me*," he replied; "why, don't you know that Man is much too clever to be killed and eaten by a Tiger? Just come with me a little way and I will show you some things which only a Man knows, but which will be very useful for you to learn."

The Tiger thought that this was a good idea, so he followed the Man through the jungle until they came to the Man's house, which was strongly built of timber and heavy logs.

"What is that place?" said the Tiger when he saw it.

"That is called a house," replied the Man. "I will show you how we use it."

And so saying he went inside and shut the door.

"Now," said he, speaking from the inside to the Tiger, "you see what a foolish creature a Tiger is compared to a Man. You poor animals live in a hole in the forest, exposed to wind, rain, cold and heat; and all your strength is of no value to make a house like this. Whereas I, although I am so much weaker than you, can build myself a fine house, where I live at my ease, indifferent to the weather and secure from the attacks of wild animals."

On hearing this the young Tiger flew into a violent passion.

"What right," said he, "has an ugly, defenceless creature like you to possess such a lovely house? Look at me, with my beautiful stripes, and my great teeth and claws, and my long tail. I am far more worthy than you of a house. Come out at once, and give your house over to me."

"Oh, very well," said the Man, and he came out of the house leaving the door open, and the Tiger stalked in.

"Now, look at me," called out the conceited young Tiger from inside, "don't I look nice in my fine house?"

"Very nice indeed," replied the Man, and bolting the door outside he walked off with his axe, leaving the Tiger to starve to death.

STORY No. III.

THE STORY OF GOOD FAITH.

THE Tiger soon got tired of sitting in the house and tried to force his way out; but the house was too strongly built for him to be able to make any impression upon the walls, so he gave it up in despair and soon began to suffer severely from hunger and thirst. Two or three days passed away and the Tiger was in a sorry state, when, as he was peering through a chink in the logs he saw a little Musk Deer, which had come down to drink at the stream which was close by. When the Tiger saw the Deer he called out to her:

"Oh, Sister Deer, will you please come and open the door of this house. I am shut up inside, and as I have nothing to eat and drink I am afraid of starving to death."

The Deer was a good deal frightened when she heard the Tiger's voice, but when she understood how matters were she was reassured, and replied:

"Oh, Uncle Tiger, I am very sorry to hear of your misfortune. But I am afraid if I open the door and let you out you will kill and eat me."

"No, no, I won't," replied the Tiger, "you can rely

upon me. I promise you faithfully that if you will release me I will let you go free."

Accordingly, the Deer came up to the house and unbolted the door from the outside, and the Tiger sprang out joyfully. As soon as he got outside he seized upon the Deer and said:

"I am very sorry for you, Sister Deer, but the fact is I am so famished that really I have no alternative but to eat you immediately."

"This is really too bad," replied the Deer; "after promising faithfully that you would not eat me, and after the benefit which I have conferred upon you, you should certainly keep faith with me."

"Faith!" said the Tiger. "What is faith? I don't believe there is any such thing as good faith."

"Is there not?" answered the Deer. "Well now, let us make a bargain. We will ask the first three living things we meet whether or no there is such a thing as good faith. If they say there is not, then you are welcome to kill and eat me; but if they say there is such a thing, then you shall let me go free."

"Very good," said the Tiger, "I agree to that; that is a bargain."

So the two set off together side by side, and after proceeding a short distance down the road they came upon a large Tree growing by the roadside.

"Good-morning, Brother Tree," said the Musk Deer, "we want to refer a question to you for your decision."

The Tree waved its branches in the air and replied in a gentle voice:

"What is your question, Sister Deer? I am ready to do my best to help you."

"The case is this," replied the Musk Deer, "a short while ago I found this Tiger shut up in a Woodcutter's hut in the forest, unable to get out. He called out to me asking me to open the door of the hut, promising me, if I did so, that he would let me go free. So I opened the door and let him out. No sooner was he released than he seized upon me and threatened to kill and eat me; and when I reproached him of breaking his faith, he said he did not believe that there was such a thing as good faith in the world. So we made a bargain that we would ask the first three living things we met whether or no there is such a thing as good faith in this world. If they say there is not, then the Tiger is to kill and eat me; but if they say that there is such a thing, then I am to go free. Will you please give us an opinion as to whether such a thing as good faith exists or not."

On hearing this story the great Tree moved its branches slowly in the breeze and replied as follows:

"I am much interested in your story, Sister Deer, and would gladly help you if I could; but I am bound to answer you honestly in accordance with my own experience of life. Now consider my own case. I grow here by the roadside and spread my branches over the dusty highway ready to give shelter to man and beast in their shade. Travellers passing constantly up and down the road avail themselves of this cool retreat, and they come themselves and they bring their poor beasts of burden to rest in my shadow. And then what happens ? Are they grateful to me for the comfort which I afford them ? Does my example inspire them with any consideration for others ? Far from it. When they have rested and refreshed themselves enough, they proceed on their way, and not only do they not thank me for my hospitality, but they break off my tender branches and use them as whips, further to goad and distress their weary animals. Can such conduct as that be called good faith ? No, I am bound to say that my experience of life leads me to believe that there is no such thing as good faith in this world."

The poor Musk Deer was much cast down on hearing these words, and she and the Tiger moved on together till, a little farther along the road, they caught sight of a Cow Buffalo and her Calf grazing quietly in a field of succulent grass. They noticed that the old Cow contented herself with the driest and smallest patches of grass, whilst showing her Calf where to find the richest and most luxuriant pasture, and that she willingly deprived herself of any comfort in order to afford pleasure to the youngster. The Tiger and the Deer approached the old Cow, and the Deer, addressing her said :

"Good-morning, Aunt Buffalo! This Tiger and I have a small matter which we wish to refer to you for an opinion."

The Buffalo gazed at them with her big eyes, and after ruminating for a while she replied slowly :

"Say on, Sister Deer, I am ready to give you my opinion for what it is worth."

"Well," said the Deer, "this Tiger was shut up in a hut in the forest, and being unable to open the door, he was in danger of starving to death. I happened to pass by, and he called to me, asking me to let him out, promising that if I did so he would spare my life. So I opened the door and released him. But no sooner was he free than he seized upon me and said that he would kill and eat me; and when I reproached him with his bad faith, he replied that he did not believe that such a thing as good faith existed. So we made a bargain that we would ask the first three living things we met whether or no they believed that there is such a thing as good faith. If they say there is not, then the Tiger is to eat me; but if they say that there is such a thing, I am to go free. Now, will you please give us your opinion on the matter."

On hearing this statement the old Buffalo continued to chew the cud for some minutes, and then replied gravely:

"I would gladly help you in the matter, Sister Deer, if I could; but I must regard it from the point of view of my own experience in life. I am considering the case of myself and my Calf. While the Calf is young and tender, I do all in my power to nourish and care for it. I first give it my milk, and later on, as you see, I encourage it to browse upon the best of the herbage, whilst I gladly stint myself in order that it may have plenty of the best of everything. But what happens later on, when the Calf grows strong and lusty? Does it remember its old mother with gratitude, and fend for her in her old age? Far from it. As soon as it is big enough it will push me away from the places where I am grazing and take the best for itself, and will drive me away altogether from the pastures if it can. Can that be called keeping faith with its mother? No; my experience makes me believe that there is no such thing as good faith in this world."

When the Musk Deer heard this she was much downhearted, and fully expected to be killed and eaten without further delay; but she begged the Tiger to give her one more chance, saying that she was fully prepared to abide by the opinion of the third person whom they met.

The Tiger consented to this, and after going on a little farther together they met a Hare, hopping quietly down the road towards them.

"Good-morning, Brother Hare," called out the Musk Deer; "could you spare us a few moments to give us an opinion upon a point of difference which has arisen between this Tiger and myself?"

"Certainly," replied the Hare, stopping short in the roadway. "I shall be delighted to do the best I can for you."

"Well," replied the Musk Deer, "the facts are as follows: I was drinking just now at a stream in the forest when I noticed this Tiger shut up in a Woodcutter's hut. The door was bolted outside, and he was unable to come out, and was in danger of starving to death, so he called out to me, asking me to release him, promising me, if I did so, that he would spare my life. I accordingly opened the door; but no sooner did the Tiger come out, than he seized upon me, saying that he was so hungry that he had really no alternative but to devour me on the spot. And when I reproached him for his bad faith, he replied that he did not know what good faith was, and, in fact, did not believe that such a thing existed. So we made a bargain that we would ask the first three living creatures we met whether or no there is such a thing as good faith in this world. If they say there is, then I am to go free; but if they say there is not, then the Tiger is at liberty to kill and eat me. We have already consulted two persons in the matter, and they are both of opinion that there is no such thing as good faith. You are the third and last, and on your decision depends my life."

"Dear me," replied the Hare, "this is a very strange story, and before giving an opinion on so momentous a matter it is necessary that I should understand exactly how it all happened. Let me see. You say that you were shut up in the Woodcutter's hut."

"No, no," broke in the Tiger; "it was I who was shut up in the Woodcutter's hut."

"Oh! I see," said the Hare; "then the Musk Deer must have shut you in?"

"Oh! no," interrupted the Musk Deer. "You don't seem to understand at all; that was not how it happened."

"Well," said the Hare, "it is such a complicated story that it is difficult to follow it exactly. So before giving a decision I propose that we all adjourn to the scene of action, and there you can explain to me precisely what occurred."

The Tiger and the Musk Deer agreed to this, and the three set off together until they arrived at the Wood-cutter's hut in the forest.

"Now," said the Hare, "will you please explain to me exactly what happened. Where, for instance, were you, Sister Deer, at the time the Tiger spoke to you?"

"I was down here drinking at the stream, so," replied the Deer, going off to the place in question.

"And where were you, Uncle Tiger?" said the Hare.

"Well, I was inside the hut, thus," replied the Tiger, going inside the house.

"And the door, I presume, must have been shut, so?" said the Hare. And so saying he shut the door and bolted it; and he and the Deer went on their way safely, leaving the Tiger shut up inside, where he shortly after starved to death.

STORY No. IV.

THE STORY OF THE TWO NEIGHBOURS.

ONCE upon a time there were two Neighbours living in two houses, side by side, in the same village. One of these was rich, and the other one poor. The rich man, whose name was Tse-ring, was proud, arrogant, and stingy; whilst the poor man, whose name was Cham-ba, was a kind-hearted man, who was generous to all as far as his means allowed.

Now it happened that a pair of Sparrows came and built their nest in the eaves over the doorway of the poor man's house, where, in the course of time, the young birds were hatched out. One day, before the young birds had learnt to fly, the two old Sparrows were away hunting for food, and one of the young ones fell out of its nest on to the poor man's door-step, and broke its leg. Shortly after the poor man coming into his house saw the young Sparrow lying helpless on his door-step, so he picked it up to see what was wrong, and found that its leg was broken. So he carried it into the house, and very carefully bound up its leg with a piece of thread; and then took it up to the roof, and put it back in the nest.

Now this Sparrow, although the poor man did not know it, was really a fairy in disguise, and later on, when it had grown up, it flew out one day and returned with its beak full of grain. The poor man was sitting in his house when the little Sparrow flew in and perched on the table in front of him. It dropped the grain on the table, and after giving one or two chirps it said to the man :

" This grain is in return for your kindness to me. Plant it in your garden and see what comes up," and so saying it flew away.

The poor man was very much surprised at hearing the Sparrow speak, and he thought to himself :

" Well, this is not a very valuable present, but still it shows how grateful even a little bird can be for a kindness done to him ; and any way I will plant the grain in my garden as it directed."

So he planted the grain just in front of his house, and soon forgot all about the incident.

A month or two later the grain grew, and soon attained its full height; and one day the poor man, going to look at it, was astonished to find that, instead of grain, each ear of corn contained a valuable jewel. He was very much delighted at this discovery, and having collected all the jewels, he carried them away to a neighbouring town, where he was able to sell them for a large sum of money, and thus found himself in a condition of great comfort and prosperity.

Soon after this the rich Neighbour, having observed the change which had taken place in the poor man's circumstances, came over one day in order to try and find out how Cham-ba had become so rich and prosperous. He carried over with him a jug of beer, and, on the pretence of conviviality, he offered his Neighbour a drink, and during the course of the conversation which followed he asked Cham-ba to tell him the secret of his new wealth. Cham-ba, who was of a very unsuspicious nature, related to him the whole story of the Sparrow, the grain, and the jewels, and having learnt the secret the rich man returned to his own house, pondering deeply how he could turn this story to his own advantage.

Now it happened that a Sparrow had hatched out her young in a nest just over his house door also. So next day he went up on to the roof, and leaning out over the parapet he picked out a young Sparrow from the nest with a pair of chop-sticks, and dropped it on to the ground below, where the poor little bird broke its leg. He then went down, picked up the young Sparrow, bound up its leg with a piece of thread, and put it back into its nest, saying as he did so that he hoped it would remember his kindness.

Sure enough, when the Sparrow grew up it flew into his house one day, and perched on the table before him. It dropped some grain from its beak, and after a few preliminary chirps it said:

"This grain is a present in return for your kindness to me. Plant it in your garden and see what grows up."

The rich man was greatly delighted on hearing this,

THE WICKED NEIGHBOUR REMOVING YOUNG SPARROW FROM NEST.

Page 22.

and thought to himself that he would soon be the possessor of beautiful jewels like his Neighbour. He prepared a bed very carefully in his garden, and planted the grain in the richest part of the soil. Every day he used to go and watch the spot, carefully examining the young shoots to see how they were getting on.

The seeds sprouted and grew very fast, and one morning, when he went out as usual to see how his crop was doing, to his astonishment he found that instead of a few stalks of barley, as he had expected, a great fierce-looking man, with a bundle of papers under his arm, was standing in the middle of the bed. The rich man was very frightened at seeing this truculent-looking stranger, and asked who he was.

"I was a creditor of yours in one of your former existences," replied the Apparition. "You were then heavily in my debt, and I have come back here with all the necessary documents to claim what you owed me."

So saying, the Stranger seized upon the rich man's house, his cattle, his sheep, his lands, and all his possessions, and reduced the rich man to the position of a slave in his household.

Some months after, Cham-ba, now rich and prosperous, started off on a journey, and before going he asked Tse-ring to take charge of a bag of gold-dust for him, and to keep it until he returned. Tse-ring undertook the charge of the gold, but in his new state of poverty and dependence he was unable to resist the temptation of spending some of it, and at last he found that the whole of the gold left in his charge was exhausted. Not knowing what to do he filled the bag with sand, and awaited his Neighbour's return with some trepidation.

A few days after Cham-ba came back from his journey, and called upon his Neighbour, and asked for his bag of gold. Tse-ring produced the bag and handed it over to Cham-ba without saying anything, and when Cham-ba opened it to see whether the gold was all right he found that it contained sand instead of gold.

"How is this?" said he. "I entrusted to you a bag of gold-dust, and you have given me back only sand."

The dishonest Neighbour had no reply to make. He pretended to look very surprised, and all he could say was:

"My friend, it has turned into this! My friend, it has turned into this!"

Cham-ba said nothing more, but carried off the bag to his own house.

Soon afterwards Cham-ba announced his intention of starting a school for little boys, where they would be taught free, and Tse-ring, thinking that a free education for his Son was not to be neglected, sent over his young Son to attend the school. A few days later he found it necessary to make a short journey to a neighbouring town, and before starting he entrusted his little Son to his neighbour, Cham-ba, and asked him to look after the boy until his return.

As soon as he was gone Cham-ba procured a tame Monkey and taught it to say the following words.

"WORTHY FATHER. I AM TURNED INTO THIS."

"Worthy father, I am turned into this! Worthy father, I am turned into this!"

When Tse-ring returned from his journey he walked over to the school-house one day to see how his Son was getting on, and he found Cham-ba seated there teaching the boys their lessons. Tse-ring looked round to see his Son, but could not detect him anywhere, but to his surprise he noticed a Monkey seated on one of the benches.

"Where is my son?" asked Tse-ring, "and how is he getting on?"

Cham-ba said nothing, but picked up the Monkey and carried it to him.

"What do you mean by this?" said Tse-ring. "This is not my Son. Where is the boy whom I entrusted to your care?"

Whereupon the Monkey spoke up and said:

"Worthy father, I am turned into this! Worthy father, I am turned into this!"

The father flew into a violent rage and stormed at his neighbour, Cham-ba, for some time, but without producing any impression. Finally, on thinking the matter over, he decided it was better to pay up the gold he had stolen, on condition of having his proper Son restored to him.

STORY No. V.

THE STORY OF THE CAT AND THE MICE.

ONCE upon a time there was a Cat who lived in a large farm-house in which there was a great number of Mice. For many years the Cat found no difficulty in catching as many Mice as she wanted to eat, and she lived a very peaceful and pleasant life. But as time passed on she found that she was growing old and infirm, and that it was becoming more and more difficult for her to catch the same number of Mice as before; so after thinking very carefully what was the best thing to do, she one day called all the Mice together, and after promising not to touch them, she addressed them as follows:

"Oh! Mice," said she, "I have called you together in order to say something to you. The fact is that I have led a very wicked life, and now, in my old age, I repent of having caused you all so much inconvenience and annoyance. So I am going for the future to turn over a new leaf. It is my intention now to give myself up entirely to religious contemplation and no longer to molest you, so henceforth you are at liberty to run about as freely as you will without fear of me. All I ask of you is that twice every day you should all file past me in procession and each one make an obeisance as you pass me by, as a token of your gratitude to me for my kindness."

When the Mice heard this they were greatly pleased, for they thought that now, at last, they would be free from all danger from their former enemy, the Cat. So they very thankfully promised to fulfil the Cat's conditions, and agreed that they would file past her and make a salaam twice every day.

So when evening came the Cat took her seat on a cushion at one end of the room, and the Mice all went by in single file, each one making a profound salaam as it passed.

Now the cunning old Cat had arranged this little plan very carefully with an object of her own; for, as soon as the procession had all passed by with the exception of one little Mouse, she suddenly seized the last Mouse in her claws without anybody else noticing what had happened, and devoured it at her leisure. And so twice every day, she seized the last Mouse of the series, and for a long time lived very comfortably without any trouble at all in catching her Mice, and without any of the Mice realising what was happening.

Now it happened that amongst these Mice there were two friends, whose names were Rambé and Ambé, who were very much attached to one another. Now these two were much cleverer and more cunning than most of the others, and after a few days they noticed that the number of Mice in the house seemed to be decreasing very much, in spite of the fact that the Cat had promised not to kill any more. So they laid their heads together and arranged a little plan for future processions. They agreed that Rambé was always to walk at the very front of the procession of the Mice, and that Ambé was to bring up the rear, and that all the time the procession was passing, Rambé was to call to Ambé, and Ambé to answer Rambé at frequent intervals. So next evening, when the procession started as usual, Rambé marched along in front, and Ambé took up his position last of all. As soon as Rambé had passed the cushion where the Cat was seated and had made his salaam, he called out in a shrill voice.

" Where are you, Brother Ambé ? "

" Here I am, Brother Rambé," squeaked the other from the rear of the procession. And so they went on calling and answering one another until they had all filed past the Cat, who had not dared to touch Ambé as long as his brother kept calling to him.

The Cat was naturally very much annoyed at having to go hungry that evening, and felt very cross all night. But she thought it was only an accident which had brought the two friends, one in front and one in rear of the procession, and she hoped to make up for her enforced abstinence by finding a particularly fat Mouse at the end of the procession next morning. What, then, was her amazement and disgust when she found that on the following morning the very same arrangement had been made, and that Rambé called to Ambé, and Ambé answered Rambé until all the Mice had passed her by, and so, for the second time, she was foiled of her meal. However, she disguised her feelings of anger and decided to give the Mice one more trial; so in the evening she took her seat as usual on the cushion and waited for the Mice to appear.

Meanwhile, Rambé and Ambé had warned the other Mice to be on the lookout, and to be ready to take flight the moment the Cat showed any appearance of anger. At the appointed time the procession started as usual, and as soon as Rambé had passed the Cat he squeaked out:

"Where are you, Brother Ambé?"

"Here I am, Brother Rambé," came the shrill voice from the rear.

This was more than the Cat could stand. She made a fierce leap right into the middle of the Mice, who, however, were thoroughly prepared for her, and in an instant they scuttled off in every direction to their holes. And before the Cat had time to catch a single one the room was empty and not a sign of a Mouse was to be seen anywhere.

After this the Mice were very careful not to put any further trust in the treacherous Cat, who soon after died of starvation owing to her being unable to procure any of her customary food; whilst Rambé and Ambé lived for many years, and were held in high honour and esteem by all the other Mice in the community.

STORY No. VI.

THE STORY OF THE FOOLISH YOUNG MUSSULMAN.

THERE was once a young Mussulman, who lived with his poor mother in a small cottage on the outskirts of a large town. As the Boy grew up, it was found that he was rather weak-minded, and that he was continually getting himself into scrapes, owing to his own folly and carelessness; and the naughty boys of the neighbourhood used to take advantage of the poor young fellow, and were constantly teasing him and telling him all sorts of absurd stories.

It chanced one day that he went for a walk in a large meadow, where there were a number of yellow flowers, and presently sitting down to rest, he began to gather a nosegay, when a young man passing by called out to him:

"Hullo! what are you doing there? Do you know that the soles of your feet are all yellow, and that is a sure sign that you are going to die at once?"

The poor young fellow was greatly frightened at hearing this, and he thought to himself:

"Well, if I am going to die, I had better have a grave ready."

So he set to work, and soon scraped out for himself a shallow grave in the soft soil. As soon as it was ready, he lay down in it and resigned himself to death.

A few minutes later one of the King's Servants, who happened to be passing by carrying an earthen jar full of oil for the King's palace, noticed the Boy lying on his back in the shallow grave, so he stopped and asked him what he was doing. The Boy replied:

"The soles of my feet are turning yellow, and that, as you know, is a sure sign that I am going to die; so I have prepared myself a grave, and am just waiting here till death comes."

"Oh, nonsense!" replied the Servant; "you could not talk like that if you were really dying. Come, get up, and help me to carry this jar of oil for the King, and I will give you a hen for yourself."

So the foolish Boy got up out of his grave, and taking the jar of oil on his back, he walked along the road with the King's Servant towards the palace. As they went along, he kept thinking to himself what he should do with his hen when he got it.

"As soon as I have got some eggs," thought he to himself, "I shall set the hen to hatch them. And then I shall have a nice lot of chickens. And when the chickens grow up into cocks and hens I shall sell them in the market. And with the money I get I shall buy a cow. And presently the cow will have a calf. And when the calf grows big I shall sell both the cow and the calf. And with the money I get I shall buy a nice little house. And when I have settled down in my house I shall marry a wife. And after a time we shall have a child. And as the child grows big I shall have to take its education in hand. And I shall be very firm and judicious with it. And if it is a good child and does what I tell it, I shall be very kind to it. And if it is naughty and does not do what it is told, I shall be very stern and stamp my foot, so!"

And thus thinking he stamped his foot so violently that the jar of oil slipped off his back and was smashed to pieces on the ground. When he saw this, the King's Servant became very angry, and asked him what on earth he meant by stamping his foot like that, and breaking a valuable jar of oil, which was intended for the King. The Boy tried to explain how it occurred, but the Servant would not listen, and dragged him off by force into the King's presence.

When the King saw them coming in together, he asked his Servant what he wanted, and why he was bringing in a strange Boy with him. The Servant replied that he had entrusted the Boy with a jar of oil intended for the King, and as they were walking along the road quite quietly together, the Boy all of a sudden began to stamp his feet like a maniac, and the jar of oil slipped off his back and got broken. The King asked the Boy what he meant by his conduct, and the Boy replied:

"Well, Your Majesty, your Servant said that if I would carry this jar of oil, he would give me a hen, and it seemed to me quite natural to consider within myself what I should do with my hen when I got it. So I soon saw that by selling the chickens I could buy a cow, and that later on by selling the cow and her calf, I could get a wife and set up a house of my own, and that presently we should have a child; and I was thinking to myself how I should keep my child in order, and if it was naughty I should be obliged to stamp my foot very firmly, in order to show it that I was not to be trifled with."

On hearing this ridiculous story the King was much amused, and laughed very heartily; and he gave the foolish Boy a piece of gold, and told him to go home to his Mother.

So the Boy went off towards his own home, and as he got near to the house he saw a strange dog sneaking out of the door, carrying in his mouth a purse full of money, which he had just picked up inside. On seeing this the Boy became very much excited, and began calling aloud to his Mother that a dog was making off with her purse. The Mother, when she found what was up, was afraid that he would attract the attention of the neighbours to the loss of the purse, and that in the excitement some one else would chase the dog and get the money; so hastily running up on to the flat roof of the house she sprinkled some sugar over the roof, and then called to the Boy to come up as quickly as he could.

"Look!" she said, as soon as he arrived; "what a curious thing! It has been raining sugar all over the roof of the house."

Her son, who was very fond of sugar, at once set to work to pick up all that he saw; and while he was so engaged, the good woman slipped away and soon found the dog and recovered her purse.

Some time afterwards the Boy's Mother arranged with a rich family, who lived some miles away, and who were not acquainted with her son's failings, that the Boy should marry the daughter of the house; and that, in accordance with Tibetan custom, he should become a member of the Bride's family. When all the preliminaries had been satisfactorily arranged, a party of horsemen arrived from the Bride's house to greet the Bridegroom and to bring him home. The Boy dressed himself up in his best clothes, and, after feasting the wedding party in the usual manner, he begged them all to go on ahead of him, saying that he would follow as soon as he had said good-bye to his Mother.

Towards evening he set out by himself on horseback. It was a moonlight night, and as he rode down the road he could see his own shadow travelling along beside him. He could not make out what the shadow was, but thought it must be some ghost or demon, which wanted to do him an injury, so he urged his horse into a gallop, in order to try and get away from it. But the faster he galloped the faster went the shadow, and he soon saw that it was no good trying to escape. So in order to frighten the strange object he took off his puggaree and flung it at it. As this produced no effect, he followed up the puggaree with his cloak, and, finally, with all the clothes he had on, but without in any way frightening the shadow, which still continued to follow him closely. So thinking to give it the slip, he jumped

THE YOUNG MUSSULMAN PURSUED BY HIS OWN SHADOW.

Page 35.

off his horse and ran along the road on foot, until he got into the shade of a big poplar-tree growing near the road-side.

Here he stopped to take breath, and he noticed to his great joy that the shadow had disappeared; but on peeping out from the shadow of the tree he was annoyed to find that on whichever side he looked the shadow immediately showed itself also. So thinking that the shade of the tree was the safest place to stay in, he climbed into the upper branches and very soon fell fast asleep.

A short while after a party of travellers happened to be passing by this road from the same direction, and as they came along they were surprised to find a number of garments scattered about the roadway. So they picked them up as they came along, and presently they found a horse grazing beside the road. Him, too, they brought along with them, and when they arrived in the shade of the poplar-tree, they all stopped and sat down on the ground to divide the spoil amongst them.

Just then the Boy woke up, and looking down he saw what was going on below, so he called out in a loud voice:

"I say, I want my share too, you know."

On hearing this voice emerging from the upper branches of the tree, the travellers were greatly alarmed. They thought it must certainly be a demon, who lived in the tree, and who wanted his share of the spoils, so they took to their heels and made off as fast as they could, leaving the horse and all the clothes behind them. The Boy then climbed down from the tree, put on his own clothes, and, mounting his horse, rode off to his Bride's house.

When he arrived at the house the parents of his Bride hurried out to greet him, and after asking him why he was so late, they led him to the room where the wedding feast was laid out. All the friends and neighbours from round about were gathered there ready to share in the feast, and to offer their congratulations to the Bride and Bridegroom.

During the progress of the feast the young Mussulman, who was of a very kindly disposition, and very fond of his Mother, kept thinking to himself how he could save something nice for her to eat from amongst so much plenty. So he picked from the table a narrow-mouthed copper vessel and concealed it in his lap, and whilst eating his food he every now and then dropped into it some particularly succulent dainty, which he thought his Mother would enjoy. Presently, however, he inadvertently thrust his hand right into the vessel, and to his horror he found that he was unable to withdraw it again. In this awkward predicament he was unable to eat anything, and the Bride's parents noticing that he no longer partook of any food, kept pressing him to have a little more. The young Man was still hungry, but was obliged to refuse all their offers, saying that he had already eaten enough.

Towards evening, when the feast was completed, the guests withdrew, and the Boy was left alone with his Bride; and she began asking him what the matter was, and why he had been behaving so strangely during the banquet.

He was at first too shy to tell her what had happened, but after much coaxing she elicited from him the fact that his right hand was confined in the neck of the copper vessel.

" Never mind," said she ; " there is a large white stone lying at the foot of the staircase. You had better slip down stairs in the dark, and by beating the vessel against the stone you will soon succeed in freeing yourself."

The young fellow thought this was a good idea, and he went off quietly down the staircase, until he detected what he thought was a white stone lying near the foot of the steps. So, creeping up to it, he raised his arm and brought down the copper vessel with great force upon the white object, shattering the vessel and leaving his hand free. But to his horror the stone, instead of being hard, gave way, and a muffled groan issued from it ; and on examining the spot, he found that instead of striking a stone, he had delivered a violent blow upon the grey head of his Bride's father, who, overcome by his potations during the wedding feast, had fallen asleep at the foot of the stairs.

The young Man was terrified at what he had done, and feeling sure that he must have killed the old man, he decided to flee from the house ; so he opened the door and ran off into the night. After running for some distance he reached a neighbouring farm, where, as it happened, a large honeycomb had been left lying in the corner of the courtyard. The Boy, not knowing what it was, lay down upon this and fell fast asleep, and soon smeared himself all over with honey. Later in the night he woke up feeling very cold, and creeping into a shed close by, which was used as a storage for wool, he lay down upon the wool and slept until morning.

He woke with the first gleam of dawn, and in the early morning light he saw that he was all white and woolly, and in his simplicity he believed that, as a punishment for his wickedness in killing his father-in-law, he had been turned into a sheep. So under this impression, he ran out of the courtyard and joined a flock of sheep, which were grazing on a neighbouring hillside. He wandered about with the sheep all day, feeling very miserable, and trying to accommodate himself to the manners and customs of his new companions, and when evening came he accompanied them into the fold where they always spent the night.

About midnight some robbers came to the fold, and getting in amongst the sheep felt about for a good fat heavy one; and finally finding that the Boy was the heaviest of them all, they proceeded to carry him off. One of them hoisted him up on to his back, and they carried him along for some distance until they reached the banks of a small stream. Here they halted, and, laying him down upon the ground, they began to make preparations for cutting his throat. This trial proved rather too much for the nerves of the young Man, and forgetting his *rôle* of sheep, he called out in a shrill voice :

"Please don't kill me, kind robbers."

On hearing this the robbers were very much frightened, and ran off as fast as they could; and the Boy, thankful to have escaped from this danger, and being thoroughly worn out by the exertions and exposure of the last twenty-four hours, returned to his Bride's house. There he found that the old man, though sorely hurt, was not dead, and having explained all the circumstances of the case, he was freely forgiven, and taken back into the household.

After living for some years very happily with his Bride, he thought that he would like to make a little money for himself by trading, so having procured a good stock of merchandise he set off for India, in the hope of making a good profit on his goods. On the way he halted one evening at a large house. The Landlord received him very hospitably, and made him quite comfortable, and during the conversation which followed their evening meal the Master of the house began telling some very tall stories. Some of these stories being rather too wonderful for belief, the young Man bluntly said that he could not believe them. Thereupon the Landlord replied:

"I can prove to you that I am telling the truth by showing you a stranger thing than anything which I have hitherto related. I will bet you that when night falls a lantern will be carried into this room by a cat instead of by a servant."

The young Man was amused at his Host's boasting, and he said:

"Very well, I am prepared to bet you anything you like that this will not happen."

"Very good," said the Landlord. "If this does not happen, I will hand you over my house, my merchandise, and everything I possess; but if it does, you will forfeit all your baggage, animals and merchandise to me." And so the bet was arranged.

Now this was a regular trick of the Landlord's, who had a tame cat which had been taught to carry in a lantern in her mouth every evening just at dusk, and he was accustomed to practise this deceit upon unwary travellers, and by this means to secure their goods and whatever property they possessed.

Sure enough, just at dusk a large white cat entered the sitting-room, holding a lighted lantern in its mouth, and the unfortunate young Man was obliged to hand over to his Host everything he possessed in the world; and finding himself without money or goods he decided to stay on in the house as a servant.

After the lapse of one or two months his Wife grew anxious about him, and knowing that from the infirmity of his mind he was likely to get himself into some scrape or another, she decided to set out herself to see what had become of him. So she disguised herself as a man, and taking with her a few ponies laden with wool, she started off to follow in the tracks of her Husband.

After several days she arrived at the house where her Husband was now employed as a servant, and, meeting him in the courtyard, she learnt from him all that had happened. So she bade him hold his tongue, and she herself entered the inn, and asked for a night's lodging. During the evening the Host got talking, and in the course of the conversation he made her the same wager as he had done to her Husband some time before.

"Well," said she, "that sounds a very strange story. I can scarcely believe it possible you can have a cat so well trained as to be able to carry in a lantern. But I will think over what you say to-night, and we will see about making the bet to-morrow morning."

Next morning at breakfast she said to her Host:

"I have thought over what you said to me yesterday, and I am now prepared to make a bet with you that the cat will *not* carry a lantern into this room at dusk this evening."

So the bet was concluded upon the same terms as before, and the Lady privately told her Husband what he was to do. So in accordance with the instructions she had given him, he caught three mice, and concealed them in a little box, which he placed in the bosom of his robe. When evening approached, the Landlord and the Lady seated themselves in the supper room, waiting to see whether or no the cat would appear as expected, whilst the Husband hid himself in a corner of the courtyard, just outside the door near where the cat was accustomed to pass.

Just at dusk the cat, carrying the lantern in its mouth, began to cross the courtyard towards the door of the room where it was expected to bring the light, and when about half way across the yard the Husband released one of the mice from the box which he had hidden in his robe. The mouse scampered off across the courtyard, and the cat gave a violent start, and was on the point of pursuing it, when its training overcame its natural instincts, and it allowed the mouse to escape.

It reluctantly continued its way towards the house, and scarcely had it started to go on, when the Husband released a second mouse, which also scampered off right in front of the cat. This time it was all the cat could do to refrain from following so tempting an opportunity. It paused with great indecision, but again, its training standing it in good stead, it pursued its way towards the house.

Just as it was reaching the door of the house the third mouse was released. This was more than the cat could stand. It dropped the lantern upon the threshold, bounded across the courtyard, and seized the mouse just as it was entering its hole.

Meanwhile the Landlord and the Lady having waited until long after dark, the Landlord was reluctantly obliged to own that he had lost his bet. So he handed over to the disguised merchant, not only his own property, but also the merchandise, which he had previously won from her Husband; and the two, carrying their possessions with them, returned to their own home, where they lived happily ever afterwards.

STORY No. VII.

THE KYANG, THE FOX, THE WOLF AND THE HARE.

ONE day a hungry Wolf was roaming about in search of something to eat in the upper part of a Tibetan valley far beyond the level of cultivation,* when he came across a young Kyang† about a year old. The Wolf at once proceeded to stalk the Kyang, thinking that he would make an excellent meal off him, and just as he was about to seize upon him the Kyang, noticing his approach, addressed him as follows:

"Oh! Uncle Wolf," said he, "it is no good your eating me now; this is the spring time and after the hard winter I am still very thin. If you will wait for a few months until next autumn you will find that I shall be twice as fat as I am now and will make you a much better feast."

"Very well," said the Wolf, "I will wait until then, on condition that you meet me on this very spot in six months' time."

* Such a locality is described in the Tibetan language by a single word—a monosyllable.

† The Kyang is the wild ass of Tibet.

And so saying he galloped off in search of some other prey.

When autumn came the Wolf started off one morning to meet the Kyang at the appointed place, and as he was going across the hills he came across a Fox.

"Good-morning, Brother Wolf," said the Fox. "Where are you going to?"

"Oh!" replied the Wolf, "I am going into the valley to meet a young Kyang by appointment, as I have arranged to catch him and eat him this very day."

"That is very pleasant for you, Brother Wolf," answered the Fox; "but as a Kyang is such a large animal you will scarcely be able to eat him all by yourself. I hope you will allow me to come too and share in the spoil."

"Certainly, Brother Fox," replied the Wolf. "I shall be very glad of your company."

And so saying the two went on together. After proceeding a short distance they came across a Hare.

"Good-morning, Brother Wolf and Brother Fox," said the Hare; "where are you two going this fine morning?"

"Good-morning, Brother Hare," replied the Wolf; "I am just going off to yonder valley to keep an appointment with a fat Kyang, whom I have arranged to kill and eat this very day, and Brother Fox is coming with me to share in the spoil."

"Oh! really, Brother Wolf," said the Hare, "I wish you would allow me to come too. A Kyang is such a large animal that you can scarcely eat him all yourselves, and I am sure you will allow a small creature like me to have a little bit of the spoil."

"Certainly, Brother Hare," replied the Wolf. "We shall be glad if you will accompany us."

And so the three animals went along together towards the appointed spot. When they got near the place they saw the young Kyang waiting for them. During the summer months he had eaten a quantity of grass and had now become very fat and sleek, and was about twice as big as he had been in the spring. When the Wolf caught sight of him he was much pleased and began to lick his chops in anticipation.

"Well, Brother Kyang," said he, "here I am according to agreement, ready to kill and eat you, and I am glad to see you look so plump and well. And here are Brother Fox and Brother Hare who have come along with me to have a bit too."

And so saying the Wolf crouched down ready to spring upon the Kyang and kill him.

"Oh, Brother Wolf," called out the Hare at this moment, "just wait one moment, for I have a suggestion to make to you. Don't you think it would be a pity to kill this fine young Kyang in the ordinary way by seizing his throat, for if you do so a great deal of his blood will be wasted? I would suggest to you, instead, that it would be a very much better plan if you would strangle him, as in that case no blood would be lost, and we should derive the full benefit from his carcase."

The Wolf thought this was a good idea and he said to the Hare:

"Very well, Brother Hare, I think that is an excellent idea of yours, but how is it to be done ?"

"Oh! easily enough," answered the Hare. "There is a shepherd's encampment over there where we can borrow a rope, and then all we have to do is to make a slip-knot in the rope, put it over the Kyang's neck, and pull as hard as we can."

So they agreed that this should be done, and the Fox went off to the encampment near by and borrowed a rope from the shepherd, which he carried back to where the three other animals were standing.

"Now," said the Hare, "leave it all to me; I will show you exactly how it is to be done."

So he took the rope and made a large slip-knot at one end and two smaller slip-knots at the other end.

"Now," said he, "this is the way we must proceed: we will put this large slip-knot over the Kyang's neck, and as he is such a large heavy animal the only way to strangle him will be for us three to pull together at the other end of the rope. So you, Brother Wolf, and you, Brother Fox, can put your heads through these smaller loops, and I will seize the loose end of the rope with my teeth, and when I give the signal we will all pull together."

The other two thought this was a very good plan, and so they threw the slip-knot over the Kyang's neck, and the Wolf and the Fox put their heads through the smaller loops. When they were all ready the Hare took up his position at the end of the rope and caught hold of it with his teeth.

"Now," said he, "are you all ready ?"

"Yes, quite ready," replied the Wolf and the Fox.

"Well, then, pull," said the Hare.

So they began to pull as hard as they could.

When the Kyang felt the pull on the rope he walked forward a few paces, much to the surprise of the Wolf and the Fox, who found themselves being dragged along the ground.

"Pull, can't you!" shrieked the Wolf, as the rope began to tighten round his neck.

"Pull yourself!" shrieked the Fox, who was now beginning to feel very uncomfortable.

"Pull, all of you," called out the Hare, and so saying he let go of the end of the rope and the Kyang galloped off dragging the Wolf and the Fox after him. In a few minutes they were both strangled, and the Kyang, shaking off the rope from his neck, proceeded to graze quietly on his usual pastures, and the Hare scampered off home, feeling that he had done a good day's work.

STORY No. VIII.

THE FROG AND THE CROW.

A Crow once caught a fine fat Frog, and taking him in her bill she flew with him to the roof of a neighbouring house in order to devour him at her leisure. As she alighted on the roof of the house the Frog gave an audible chuckle.

"What are you laughing at, Brother Frog?" said the Crow.

"Oh, nothing, Sister Crow," said the Frog; "never mind me. I was just thinking to myself that, as it fortunately happens, my Father lives close by here, on this very roof, and as he is an exceedingly fierce, strong man, he will certainly avenge my death if anyone injures me."

The Crow did not quite like this, and thinking it as well to be on the safe side she hopped off to another corner of the roof near to where a gutter led away the rain water by means of a small hole in the parapet and a wooden spout. She paused here for a moment and was just about to begin to swallow the Frog when the Frog gave another chuckle.

"What are you laughing at this time, Brother Frog?" asked the Crow.

"Oh, it's only a small matter, Sister Crow, hardly worth mentioning," replied the Frog, "but it just occurred to me that my Uncle, who is even a stronger and fiercer man than my Father, lives in this very gutter, and that if anybody was to do me an injury here they would have a very small chance of escaping from his clutches."

The Crow was somewhat alarmed at hearing this, and she thought that, on the whole, it would be safer to leave the roof altogether; so again picking up the Frog in her bill she flew off to the ground below, and alighted near the edge of a well. Here she placed the Frog upon the ground and was just about to eat him when the Frog said:

"Oh, Sister Crow, I notice your bill seems rather blunt. Before you begin to eat me don't you think it would be a good thing to sharpen it a little. You can strop it very nicely on that flat stone over there."

The Crow, thinking this was a good idea, took two or three hops towards the stone, and began sharpening her bill. As soon as she had turned her back the Frog gave one desperate jump, and dived into the well.

As soon as the Crow had made her bill nice and sharp she returned from the stone, and looked about for the Frog. Not finding him where she had left him she hopped to the edge of the well and peeped over, craning her head from side to side. Presently she spied the Frog in the water, and called out to him:

"Oh, Brother Frog, I was afraid you were lost. My

bill is quite nice and sharp now, so come along up and be eaten."

"I am so sorry, Sister Crow," replied the Frog, "but the fact is, I cannot get up the sides of this well. The best thing would be for you to come down here to eat me."

And so saying he dived to the bottom of the well.

STORY No. IX.

THE HARE AND THE LIONS.

ONCE upon a time there lived a Lion and a Lioness who inhabited a den amongst some rocks on the slopes of a mountain. They were both very fine, well-grown animals, and they used to prey upon all the smaller beasts in that part of the country; until at last they became so powerful that no other animal was safe from their clutches, and the wild beasts of the neighbourhood lived in a continual state of terror.

It chanced one day that while the Lion was hunting for something to eat, he came across a Hare sleeping behind a boulder; and seizing the Hare in his great paws he was just about to devour him, when the Hare spoke as follows:

"Oh! Uncle Lion," said he, "before eating me I just want to tell you about another animal who lives in that pond down there in the valley. He is very big and fierce, and I think he must be even stronger than you are. But if you will allow me to do so I will show you where he lives, and if you can succeed in killing him he will make a very much better meal for you than a poor little beast like me."

On hearing this the Lion was very indignant.

"What!" said he, "do you mean to tell me that there is any animal in this country stronger and more powerful than I am? Don't you know that I am the Lord of this district, and that I should never allow anyone else to dispute the mastery with me. Show me at once where this creature lives, and I will show you how I shall deal with him."

"Oh! Uncle Lion," said the Hare, "let me beg you to be careful. You have no idea what a big, strong creature this is; you must on no account allow yourself to be injured by fighting with him. Think what a grief it would be to us all if you were to come to any harm."

This remark of the Hare's made the Lion more angry than before, and he insisted that the Hare should at once lead him down and show him where the other animal lived. So the Hare, after again begging him to be careful of himself, preceded him down the hill until they arrived at the edge of a square-built stone tank, which was nearly full of water.

"Now, Uncle Lion," said the Hare, "if you will go to the edge of that tank and look down into the water you will see the animal I speak of."

So saying he moved on one side, and the Lion, stalking to the edge, peered down into the tank. The water was very smooth, and on the clear surface he saw his own head reflected.

"There he is," called out the Hare from the background; "there he is, Uncle Lion, I can see him quite plainly in the water. You see how fierce he is looking; please be careful not to start fighting with him."

These remarks made the Lion more angry than ever, and he moved up and down on the brink of the tank, glaring fiercely at his own reflection in the water, and growling and showing his teeth at it.

"That's right, Uncle Lion," called out the Hare; "I am so glad you are taking good care of yourself. Don't on any account come to grips with that beast in the water or he might do you an injury. You are certainly much safer on the bank, and no doubt you will frighten him if you continue to growl and show your teeth."

These last observations of the Hare goaded the Lion to desperation, and with a fierce roar he sprang straight at the image in the water. Once in the tank he was unable to get out, for its sides were built of masonry, and it was impossible for him to climb them. So he swam about for some time in the tank, whilst the Hare, sitting on the bank, threw stones at him and made nasty remarks; and finally, when quite wearied out, he sank to the bottom and was drowned.

The Hare was very pleased at having accomplished the destruction of the Lion, and he now turned his attention to the Lioness. It happened that near by there was a thick wall standing, which was part of the remains of a ruined castle; and in one portion of the wall there was a hole, very large at one end and tapering down to quite a small opening at the other. The Hare, having studied his ground, went off next morning to find the Lioness. He soon came across her stalking up and down near her den, very much perturbed at the disappearance of her lord and master.

"Good-morning, Aunt Lioness," said the Hare, going up cautiously towards her; "what is the matter with you this morning? How is it I find you pacing here in front of your den instead of hunting your prey as usual on the hillside?"

The Lioness took no notice of the Hare, except to growl at him in an angry manner, and to lash her sides with her tail.

"I suppose," went on the Hare, "you are anxious about Mr. Lion, but I am sorry to tell you that you are not likely to see him again for some time. The fact is, he and I had a little argument yesterday, in which we both lost our tempers. It ended in our having a free fight, and I regret to say that I was obliged to injure Mr. Lion rather severely before I could make him see reason, and he is now lying in a dying state in the valley below."

This impudence so enraged the Lioness that she sprang towards the Hare and endeavoured to seize him; but he eluded her and galloped off down the hill hotly pursued by the angry beast. The Hare made straight for the ruined wall, and entering the breach in the wall at the large end he emerged safely at the other side by the smaller recess, which was just large enough for him to pass through. The Lioness, following closely at his heels, was so blind with rage that she did not see that she was being led into a trap; so she rushed head-foremost into the opening in the wall, and before she had time to stop herself was wedged tightly in the tapering hole. She struggled violently, trying to extricate herself, but all in vain.

Meanwhile the Hare, having cantered round to the other side, took up its position in rear of the Lioness, and began pelting her with stones and calling her all the bad names he could think of. When he was tired of this he went off home very pleased with himself, and the Lioness, being unable to free herself from the trap she was in, shortly afterwards starved to death.

STORY No. X.

THE SHEEP, THE LAMB, THE WOLF AND THE HARE.

ONCE upon a time there lived an old Sheep in a low-lying valley of Tibet, and every year she, with her Lamb,* were in the habit of leaving the valley during the early months of summer, and going up on to the great northern plateau, where grass is plentiful, and where many Sheep and Goats graze throughout the summer.

One spring the Sheep, in accordance with her annual custom, set out for the north, and one day, as she was strolling sedately along the path, while her little Lamb skipped about beside her, she suddenly came face to face with a large, fierce-looking Wolf.

"Good-morning, Aunty Sheep," said the Wolf; "where are you going to?"

"Oh! Uncle Wolf," replied the trembling Sheep, "we are doing no harm; I am just taking my Lamb to graze on the rich grass of the great northern plateau."

"Well," said the Wolf, "I am really very sorry for you; but the fact is, I am hungry, and it will be necessary for me to eat you both on the spot."

* This story is also told of a Sheep and a Goat, instead of a Sheep and a Lamb. See accompanying illustration.

"Please, please, Uncle Wolf, don't do that," replied the Sheep. "Please don't eat us now; but if you will wait till the autumn, when we shall both be very much fatter than we are now, you can eat us with much more benefit to yourself on our return journey."

The Wolf thought this was a good idea.

"Very well, Aunty Sheep," said he, "that is a bargain. I will spare your lives now, but only on condition that you meet me at this very spot on your return journey from the north in the autumn."

So saying, he galloped off, and the Sheep and the Lamb continued on their way towards the north, and soon forgot all about their encounter with the Wolf.

All the summer they grazed about on the succulent grass of the great plateau, and when autumn was approaching both were as fat as fat could be, and the little Lamb had grown into a fine young Sheep.

When the time came for returning to the south, the Sheep remembered her bargain with the Wolf, and every day as they drew farther and farther south she grew more and more downhearted.

One day, as they were approaching the place where they had met the Wolf, it chanced that a Hare came hopping along the road towards them. The Hare stopped to say good-morning to the Sheep, and noticing that she was looking very sad, he said:

"Good-morning, Sister Sheep, how is it that you, who are so fat and have so fine a Lamb, are looking so sad this morning?"

"Oh! Brother Hare," replied the Sheep, "mine is a very sad story. The fact is that last spring, as I and my Lamb were coming up this very road, we met an ugly-looking Wolf, who said he was going to eat us; but I begged him to spare our lives, explaining to him that we should both be much larger and fatter in the autumn, and that he would get much better value from us if he waited till then. The Wolf agreed to this, and said that we must meet him at the same spot in the autumn. We are now very near the appointed place, and I very much fear that in another day or two we shall both be killed by the Wolf."

So saying, the poor Sheep broke down altogether and burst into tears.

"Dear me! dear me!" replied the Hare; "this is indeed a sad story; but cheer up, Sister Sheep, you may leave it to me, and I think I can answer for it that I know how to manage the Wolf."

So saying, the Hare made the following arrangements. He dressed himself up in his very best clothes, in a new robe of woollen cloth, with a long ear-ring in his left ear, and a fashionable hat on his head, and strapped a small saddle on to the back of the Sheep. He then prepared two small bundles, which he slung across the Lamb, and tied them on with a rope. When these preparations were complete, he took a large sheet of paper in his hand, and, with a pen thrust behind his ear, he mounted upon the back of the Sheep, and the little procession started off down the path.

Soon after, they arrived at the place where they were

THE HARE CONVERSING WITH THE WOLF.

to meet the Wolf, and sure enough there was the Wolf waiting for them at the appointed spot.

As soon as they came within earshot of where the Wolf was standing the Hare called out in a sharp tone of authority:

"Who are you, and what are you doing there?"

"I am the Wolf," was the reply; "and I have come here to eat this Sheep and its Lamb, in accordance with a regular arrangement. Who may you be, pray?"

"I am Lomden, the Hare," that animal replied, "and I have been deputed to India on a special mission by the Emperor of China. And, by the way, I have a commission to bring ten Wolf skins as a present to the King of India. What a fortunate thing it is that I should have met you here! Your skin will do for one, anyway."

So saying, the Hare produced his sheet of paper, and, taking his pen in his hand, he wrote down the figure "1" very large.

The Wolf was so frightened on hearing this that he turned tail and fled away ignominiously; while the Sheep and the Lamb, after thanking the Hare heartily for his kind offices, continued their journey safely to their own home.

[This story is a satire on the assumption and arrogance of Tibetan and Chinese officials, and the timidity and submissiveness of the Tibetan peasants. It illustrates how the meanest Government clerk, more especially when armed with pen and paper, can strike terror into the heart of the boldest and strongest countryman.]

STORY No. XI.

THE STORY OF HOW THE HARE MADE A FOOL OF THE WOLF.

[This story is really the continuation of Number X., which is sometimes told of "the Sheep and the Goat," instead of "the Sheep and the Lamb." The first part of the story is exactly the same as Number X. They experience the same adventures with the Wolf and are extricated in exactly the same manner by the aid of the Hare. But the end of the story is different.]

When the Wolf ran away, Da-gye the Sheep and Pen-dzong the Goat were so elated that they could not refrain from vaingloriously galloping after him until they saw him dive hastily into his earth some distance away; they then sat themselves down at the mouth of the hole and remained there for some time chaffing the Wolf and telling him to hurry up and come out to be skinned, whilst the foolish Wolf lay cowering and trembling within.

Presently the Sheep grew rather hungry and thirsty, so she went off to eat and drink, leaving the Goat to watch the earth. After sitting for a short while the

Goat began rubbing his horns on a stone, and the Wolf hearing the grating sound squeaked out very humbly:

"Oh! Brother Goat, what are you doing now?"

"Sharpening a knife to kill you with," replied the Goat.

And the Wolf cowered into the furthest recesses of his den trembling with fear.

A few minutes later some rain began to fall, and the Wolf hearing the sound of the pattering raindrops called out:

"What is happening now, pray, Brother Goat?"

"I am collecting the water to cook you in," answered the Goat gruffly.

Presently the Goat began to scrape the earth with one hoof and the Wolf asked:

"What is that scraping noise, Brother Goat?"

"I am preparing a fireplace to boil the water at," answered the Goat. "It will soon be time to finish you off."

Just then the Sheep came back from grazing and said to the Goat:

"Now, Brother Goat, it is time for you to go and refresh yourself. I will stay here and look after the Wolf while you are away."

The Goat thanked the Sheep for her offer and told her how he had been acting during her absence, and after advising her to behave in the same manner and on no account to show any signs of fear, he went off to get something to eat and drink.

When the Sheep found herself left alone at the mouth of the Wolf's den, her natural timidity asserted itself, and she began to feel very nervous, but in order to keep up appearances she started to rub her horns against a stone, just as the Goat had advised her to do. As soon as he heard this noise the Wolf called out as before, asking what was happening.

"I am sharpening a knife to kill you with," replied the Sheep, but she was so nervous that the Wolf at once noticed the terrified sound of her voice and began to suspect that he had been made a fool of.

"Is that you, Sister Sheep?" said the Wolf; "I thought it was Brother Goat."

"No, Brother Wolf, it is me," replied the Sheep. "Brother Goat has gone away to get himself something to eat and drink."

"And are you all alone, Sister Sheep?" asked the Wolf.

"Yes, Brother Wolf," replied the Sheep.

On hearing this the Wolf dashed out of his den, and seizing hold of the poor Sheep he quickly slew her.

The Wolf now realised that he had been made game of by the Sheep and the Goat and became very angry. So he started off to hunt for the Goat, vowing vengeance against him. As soon as the Goat caught sight of the Wolf coming along in the distance he guessed what had happened, and fled as fast as he could across the hills with the Wolf after him. They soon came to some rough, rocky ground, and here the Goat missed his footing and fell into a deep, narrow cleft between two rocks, breaking his leg; and the Wolf, who had not seen what had happened, jumped over the crevice and pursued his way, still hunting for the Goat.

For some time the poor Goat lay helpless at the bottom of the crevice, when by chance a Fox, who happened to be passing that way, heard him moaning and came to see what was wrong.

"Good-morning, Brother Goat," said the Fox, peering down into the cleft. "What has happened to you, and why do you lie there moaning?"

"Oh! Brother Fox," replied the Goat, "I have had a terrible misfortune. I am Pen-dzong the Goat, and I and my friend Da-gye the Sheep hunted a Wolf into his lair this morning and tried to frighten him by telling him that we were going to skin him; and while I was away getting myself something to drink and eat the Wolf came out of his den and killed my poor friend Da-gye the Sheep, and then proceeded to chase me. But I, as you see, fell down into this cleft and have broken my leg. I am unable to move, and the Wolf jumped over the crevice as I lay here and has gone right away. I have one dying request to make to you, however. I beg you when I am dead to strip off my skin and to hand it over to my young ones as a mat for them to lie on, and in return for this service you can have my flesh for yourself."

The Fox was much affected on hearing the Goat's tale, and promised to do as he asked. So when the Goat died shortly after the Fox stripped off his skin, and set off with it to hand it over to the Goat's young ones. As he was going along, carrying the skin on his back, he chanced to come across a Hare.

"Good-day, Brother Fox," said the Hare. "Where are you going to, and what is that you have on your back?"

"Good-day, Brother Hare," replied the Fox. "This is the skin of Pen-dzong the Goat, whom I found lying in a cleft between two rocks with a broken leg. He and his friend Da-gye the Sheep have both been killed by a Wolf, and he begged me after his death to strip off his skin and to take it as a last present from him to his young ones.

"Dear me," replied the Hare, "that no doubt must be the same Goat and the same Sheep whom I rescued so recently from that very Wolf. What foolish creatures they are to have got themselves into so much trouble after I had freed them from all their difficulties. But, nevertheless, I am not going to let the Wolf get the best of me like this, and kill my friends with impunity. Come along with me and we will see what we can do to avenge Da-gye and Pen-dzong."

The Fox agreed to this, and he and the Hare set off together to hunt for the Wolf. They travelled a long way without coming across him, but at length, as they were crossing a high pass they found him feeding upon the carcase of a dead Horse.

"Good-day, Uncle Wolf," called out the Hare genially. "I am so glad to have met you. The fact is, there is a wedding feast going on at that big house over yonder, where Brother Fox and I expect to find plenty to eat and drink. If you care to come along with us too we shall be very glad, and I think we can promise you some better refreshment than that old Horse you are devouring here. So come along and see what we can find."

The Wolf was very pleased at this invitation, so he joined the Hare and the Fox, and all three went off together to the big house where the wedding feast was being held. They studied the premises carefully before approaching too near, and they soon ascertained that the whole of the wedding party were busy feasting in the central room, and that the larder, full of good things to eat and drink, was quite unguarded. So they jumped in through a narrow window and began to enjoy themselves thoroughly, eating and drinking anything which took their fancy. When they were as full as could be the Hare said :

"What I advise now is as follows : let us each take some provisions, as much as we can carry, and bring them with us to our own homes, so that we may have something to go on with when we next feel hungry. I myself shall take some cheese; Brother Fox no doubt would like some cold fowl ; and I should advise you, Brother Wolf, to carry off that jar of wine."

The Fox and the Wolf both agreed with the Hare's proposals, and they began to load themselves with the provisions they proposed to take with them. The Fox and the Hare had no difficulty in making up a bundle of cheese and cold fowl, but the Wolf found that it would be very difficult for him to carry off the jar of wine. So the Hare explained to him that the best plan would be for him to slip his head through the handle of the jar, in which case it would be quite easy for him to drag the jar along with him. So the Wolf put his head through the handle of the jar, and all three made ready to start.

"Well now, Brother Fox and Brother Wolf," said the Hare in a genial tone of voice, "it is nearly time for us to be off. How are you both feeling? Have you had a good dinner? Are your bellies full?"

"Couldn't be fuller," replied the Wolf, rubbing his stomach with one paw. "I have done very well."

"Well, then," said the Hare, "as we have feasted well and feel happy and contented, let's have a song before starting."

"Certainly, Brother Hare," replied the Wolf. "Will you begin?"

"I would with pleasure," answered the Hare, "but really, the fact is, I can't recollect a single song at this moment. Perhaps Brother Fox will oblige us."

"I am very sorry, Brother Hare," answered the Fox, "but I am afraid I don't know any songs. I am sure Brother Wolf sings beautifully."

"Yes," joined in the Hare. "Pray, Brother Wolf, let us hear you sing?"

"No, no, please," said the Wolf modestly, scratching his ear with one paw. "I am a very poor singer, you really must excuse me."

But the Fox and the Hare pressed him, and presently he began to sing. At the first sound of his voice the men in the next room stopped their feasting, and saying to one another, "There is a Wolf in the house," they rushed towards the larder.

As soon as they heard the disturbance the Hare and the Fox, carrying their provisions with them, hopped quietly out of the window and made off quickly for their homes. The Wolf, too, made a leap towards the window, but the great jar round his neck was too broad to go through the narrow opening, and he fell back into the room below. Again he jumped and again he fell back; and he was still jumping and falling when the people of the house rushed in and soon despatched him with sticks and stones.

STORY No. XII.

THE MOUSE'S THREE CHILDREN.

MANY years ago, in the kingdom of Nepal, there was a little Mouse, who lived with her husband in a snug nest not far from the King's palace.

Finding that she was about to be delivered of a child, the Mouse prayed to the gods that her offspring might be very strong; and when the child was born it appeared in the form of a young Tiger. The Tiger soon grew up, and one day he said to the Mouse:

"Mother, I must now go off into the jungle and live there with my brother Tigers. But if at any time you want my help, all you need do is to go into yonder thicket, and throw a handful of my hair into the air, and call my name three times."

So saying, he gave the Mouse a handful of his hair, and went off into the forest.

Shortly afterwards the Mouse was again with child, and this time she prayed that her offspring might be very beautiful. When the child was born, instead of a young Mouse, she found that she had given birth to a Peacock. The Peacock soon grew into a large and beautiful bird, and when he had reached his full growth he one day said to his mother:

"Mother, it is now time for me to go and seek my own livelihood with my brothers in the forest. But if at any time you should require my assistance, all you have to do is to go to the top of that hill over there, and to throw a handful of my feathers into the air, and call my name three times."

So saying, he gave the little Mouse a handful of his feathers, and flew away into the jungle.

Presently the Mouse found herself a third time with child, and this time she prayed to the gods that her child might become wise, wealthy and powerful; and when the child appeared she saw that it was a young man child. As the Boy grew up the mother was afraid that he, too, like his brothers, would want to leave his nest and go out into the world to live with his fellow-men. So she told him the story of his two elder brothers, and explained to him that he was a man child, and could not wander away into the jungle like they did, but must stay in the nest. The Boy promised to do so, and every day he used to sit and play about at the mouth of the nest.

Now it happened that in that country there lived a Mussulman, who made his living as a barber and by paring people's nails. This man, who was very clever at his work, was often employed in the King's palace, and one day, as he was going to his work in the palace, he passed near to the Mouse's nest. There he saw the Boy seated on the ground, and, going up to him, he asked him whether he would like his hair cut and his nails pared.

The Boy said, "Yes," and the Barber proceeded to cut his hair. To the Barber's astonishment, each hair, as it fell to the ground, immediately turned into diamonds, pearls, and other jewels; and when he proceeded to pare the Boy's nails, each paring, as it touched the ground, became a beautiful turquoise.

The Barber then went on to the palace, and as he was cutting the King's hair, he told him about the miraculous child, whose hair and nails turned into jewels. The King, who was a greedy and unscrupulous man, determined to gain possession of so valuable a Boy, so he sent out some of his servants to bring the Boy up to the palace. When the Boy arrived, he was brought before the King, and the King told him that as he had been found trespassing in the royal forests, he intended to kill the mother, and to keep the Boy as a slave, unless the Boy could furnish him at once with four full-grown Tigers to guard the four gates of the palace, in which case he would marry the Boy to his daughter and would give him half his kingdom.

The poor Boy went in great grief to Mother Mouse, and related to her the whole of his interview with the King. The Mouse told him not to vex himself, and she gave him a handful of Tiger's hair and sent him out into the jungle with full directions as to what he should do.

The Boy went off into the heart of a dense thicket in the jungle, and throwing the Tiger's hair into the air, he called out at the same time:

"Brother Tiger! Brother Tiger! Brother Tiger!"

Scarcely had the words left his lips when he heard a low, deep growl just beside him, and a great Tiger stalked out of the thicket, licking his chops.

"Here I am, Brother," said the Tiger. "What do you want?"

"Oh! Brother Tiger," said the Boy, "the King has said that if I do not immediately provide him with four full-grown Tigers to guard the four gates of his palace he will kill our mother and make me a slave."

On hearing this the Tiger laughed aloud.

"Is that all?" said he. "That is easily arranged. I can get you a hundred Tigers."

So saying, he opened his mouth, and gave forth a series of fearful roars; and in a few minutes the whole jungle seemed to be full of Tigers, hastening up from all directions. When they were all ready, the first Tiger told his brother to mount upon his back, and so, with the Boy leading the way, and the other Tigers following in procession, they all went off in a body to the King's palace.

As they approached the palace great consternation arose; servants ran hither and thither, and the guards were called to arms. And when the King was told what was happening he was greatly alarmed himself, but he seated himself on his throne, and gave orders for the Boy and the Tigers to be admitted.

The Boy rode in on the Tiger's back to the royal presence, followed by all the other Tigers; and halting a few steps from the throne he said:

"Here, oh King! are a number of the best Tigers I could find in the forest. You can take your pick of any four you like."

The King was very much astonished at this, and having

selected four of the finest Tigers, he allowed the others to go away. But he still hankered after the jewels, and in a few days' time he again summoned the Boy before him, and told him that unless he at once furnished four Peacocks to sit one on each of the four golden pinnacles of his palace roof, he should kill his mother and keep the Boy as a slave.

The poor Boy was very down-hearted on hearing this, and went sadly back to his mother with the news; but the little Mouse told him that it was all right, and giving him a handful of Peacock's feathers, she instructed him how to proceed. So the Boy went off to the top of a high hill, and, throwing the feathers into the air, he called aloud:

"Brother Peacock! Brother Peacock! Brother Peacock!"

Immediately a fluttering sound was heard, and a magnificent Peacock dropped to the ground in front of him from the branch of a neighbouring tree.

"Here I am, Brother," said the Peacock. "What do you want with me?"

"Oh! Brother Peacock," said the Boy, "the King says that if I cannot at once provide him with four Peacocks to sit on the four golden pinnacles of his palace, he will kill our mother and make me a slave."

"Never mind," said the Peacock, "we can easily arrange that."

So he fluttered back to the top of a high tree, and called the loud, shrill call of the Peacocks.

In a few moments the air was bright with numbers of fine Peacocks flying in from all directions.

"Now," said the first Peacock, "come along to the palace."

So saying, four of the strongest Peacocks seized the Boy in their claws, and they all flew together over the tops of the trees to the King's palace.

When the courtiers saw the Peacocks coming, they ran to tell the King, and the King seated himself upon his throne in the courtyard all ready to receive them.

The Peacocks placed the Boy upon the ground in front of the King's throne, and arranged themselves in rows behind him, with their tails spread.

"Here, oh King!" said the Boy, "are all the finest Peacocks I could find in the forest. You can have your pick of any four of them."

The King was greatly astonished at what had happened, but he selected the four best Peacocks, and sent away the rest.

But the King still hankered in his heart after the jewels. So, a few days later, he sent for the Boy again, and he told him that unless his Mother Mouse could fight single-handed with the King's state Elephant and destroy it, he would kill the mother and make the Boy a slave.

The Boy was greatly distressed on hearing this, for he did not think it possible that the little Mouse could compete successfully with the King's great Elephant; so he went home very sadly and told his mother the whole story. But the Mouse told him he was not to be alarmed, and she directed him to smear her body all over with poison, and to tie a long string to her tail. As soon as she was ready the Boy placed her in the sleeve of his coat, and carried her along to the palace.

In the courtyard of the palace everything had been made ready for the fight. Seats had been prepared behind a barrier for the King and his nobles, whilst the roofs and the windows were crowded with hundreds of people who had come to see the show. At one end of the enclosure the King's great tusker stood ready, still chained by the leg; and the Boy, with the Mouse in his sleeve, took up his stand at the other end of the arena, face to face with the angry Elephant.

At a given signal the Elephant's chain was loosed, and with a bellow of rage he rushed towards where the Boy was standing. As he came on, holding his trunk high in the air, the little Mouse jumped to the ground and ran to meet him. The Elephant caught sight of this small object, and stopped for a moment to see what it was, and the Mouse hopped on to his foot. The Elephant at once put down his trunk to feel what was there, and in a twinkling the Mouse jumped into the open end of the trunk, and scuttled up it as fast as she could till she reached the head. She soon found herself inside the Elephant's brain, and there she ran round and round, smearing poison all over the brain of the great beast.

The Elephant, not knowing what had happened, rushed round the arena, bellowing with rage and pain, and smashing everything within reach of his trunk. But presently, the poison taking effect, he fell to the ground stone dead, and the Boy, pulling the string which was attached to the Mouse's tail, guided her out of the Elephant's trunk till she reached the open air.

The King could no longer hesitate to fulfil his promise to the Boy, so he gave him his daughter in marriage, and presented him with half his kingdom. And on the King's death the Boy succeeded to the kingdom, and he and his mother lived happily ever afterwards.

STORY No. XIII.

THE JACKALS AND THE TIGER.

ONCE upon a time there was a family of Jackals, consisting of a Father, Mother, and five young ones. After living for some time very comfortably near a large village, they found that the dogs of the village were becoming so numerous and so troublesome that they considered it necessary to change their place of abode. So one fine evening they started off and travelled away across the country, keeping a sharp look-out for some desirable spot in which they might settle down.

After a while they came to the edge of a forest, and having travelled for some little distance into the thickest part of the wood, they arrived all of a sudden at a Tiger's den. The young Jackals were a good deal frightened at the smell of the Tiger's den, but Father Jackal reassured them, and said that he thoroughly understood Tigers, and knew how to deal with them. So he went forward alone, and, peeping in, he found that the Tiger was out, but that he had left a large quantity of deer's flesh lying in one corner, which apparently he had not had time to consume. So he called Mrs. Jackal and the children, and told them to go inside and to have a good feed, and to make themselves quite comfortable. After making a good meal himself off the deer's flesh, he said to Mrs. Jackal:

"You and the children can now go to sleep; I shall go on to the roof of the den and keep a look-out for the Tiger. When I see him coming I shall rap on the roof, and you must at once wake up the children and make them begin to cry, and when I ask you what they are crying about, you must say that they are getting impatient for their supper."

Accordingly Mr. Jackal went up on the roof, while his family settled down to sleep in the snuggest corner of the Tiger's den. Shortly after Father Jackal heard a slight crackling amongst the dry leaves of the forest; and in the dim morning light he discerned the form of a great Tiger approaching his den through the tree-stems.

According to the arrangement he had made, he rapped with a loose stone upon the roof of the den, and Mrs. Jackal immediately woke up the young Jackals and made them cry.

"What are those children crying about?" called out Father Jackal.

"They are very hungry, and getting impatient for their supper," was the reply.

"Tell them they won't have long to wait now," said Father Jackal; "the Tiger will probably be home very soon, and we shall all be eating hot Tiger's meat before long."

On hearing this the Tiger was very much alarmed, and thought to himself:

"What kind of strange animal can this be which has

entered my den, and is waiting to cook and eat me on my return; it must certainly be a very fierce and terrible creature."

So without waiting to investigate the matter any further, he turned tail and ran off as fast as he could through the forest. After running some way, he came across an old Baboon, with a great fringe of white hair all round his face.

"Where are you running to, Uncle Tiger?" asked the Baboon.

"Well," said the Tiger, "the fact is, that a family of strange animals, who call themselves Jackals, are at this moment in occupation of my den. As I was approaching my den, after a long night's hunting, one of the creatures was actually sitting on the roof, looking out for me, and as I got close up I heard him tell his young ones that they were to have hot Tiger's meat for supper. Fortunately for me, he hadn't seen me, so I thought the best thing I could do was to make off as fast as I could, in order to avoid being eaten."

On hearing this the Baboon was very much amused, and set to work to laugh very heartily.

"Why," said he, "what a foolish Tiger you are! Have you never heard of a Jackal before? Don't you know that it is you should eat the Jackals, and not the Jackals you? You come along with me, and I will soon show you how to deal with people like that."

The Tiger was somewhat reassured on hearing what the Baboon had to say, but, even so, he was at first very reluctant to return again and to incur the danger of being

THE TIGER AND THE MONKEY APPROACHING THE JACKAL'S DEN.

eaten; but the Monkey encouraged him, and finally they set off together, the Monkey twisting his tail round the Tiger's, in order to give him a feeling of support and confidence.

As they came nearer to the den, the Tiger grew more and more timorous, and would only advance very slowly, ready to take flight at any moment. However, they went on together, tail-in-tail, until presently Father Jackal on the roof of the den caught sight of the pair, and called out:

"That is right, Brother Monkey, bring him along quickly; we are all half starved. But what do you mean by only bringing one of them? I had expected you would bring us at least two or three."

On hearing this, the Tiger at once suspected that the Baboon was in the Jackal's employ, and that he was being led into a trap. Without a moment's hesitation he turned about and fled precipitately into the depths of the forest. The unfortunate Baboon, whose tail was tightly twisted round the Tiger's, was unable to free himself, and was dragged and bumped hither and thither in the Tiger's rush through the thickest and thorniest parts of the jungle. When at length the Tiger paused, many miles away, to take breath, he looked back at his flanks, and all he saw of the Monkey was a bit of its tail which had broken off and was still twisted round his own.

He never again returned to his den, which was occupied henceforth by the Jackals, who lived there for many years in peace and comfort.

STORY No. XIV.

THE STORY OF THE THREE THIEVES.

ONCE upon a time there lived within the dominions of the Emperor of China three very clever Thieves. These men, owing to their skill and cunning, were quite at the head of their profession, and by sleight of hand and dexterity were able to accomplish feats of trickery which the ordinary thieves could not emulate. The first was so clever that he was able to withdraw eggs from under a sitting hen without in any way disturbing her, and without her being aware that the theft had been accomplished. The second was able to cut the soles off a man's boots as he walked along the road without the victim knowing that he had been robbed. And the third was able to eat his fill off a man's plate during dinner without the man who was robbed, or his friend opposite, being able to detect where the victuals had gone to.

Now it happened one day that these three Thieves met together in a country inn, and entering into conversation with one another, began to exchange confidences.

"May I ask what you do for a living?" asked the first Thief of the second.

"Oh, I am a Thief," answered the man who was addressed.

"Very good," replied the other men, "we also are Thieves. Can you tell us, please, if there is any particular line in which you excel?"

"Yes," said the second Thief; "I am able to cut the soles off a man's boots as he walks across the road without his being aware of what has happened. What can you two do, pray?"

"I," replied the first Thief, "can withdraw the eggs from under a sitting hen without disturbing her."

"And I," said the third, "can steal another man's dinner from off his plate, and eat my fill as he sits at table, without the victim, or the man sitting opposite, being able to detect me."

So the three Thieves, having struck up a friendship on the ground of their unusual skill, set off together to the court of the Emperor of China, in order to see whether they could not succeed in making their fortunes there.

On arriving at the court they consulted together and came to the conclusion that in order to make any headway in China it was necessary to attract the attention of the Emperor. So they agreed to separate for twenty-four hours, and to meet next day in the courtyard of the palace, each bringing some gift to the Emperor which would please him, and prove to him that they were men of no usual calibre. Accordingly, they parted in different directions, and the following day at noon, they met together in the courtyard of the palace, and each one proceeded to relate his adventures during the preceding twenty-four hours.

"As soon as I left you yesterday," began the first Thief, "I went into the royal farm adjoining the palace, and there I found one of the Emperor's pea-hens sitting upon her nest, and hatching a clutch of eggs, which was calculated to produce a breed of the very finest peacocks. By the Emperor's orders this nest was watched by an attendant night and day, in order that no one should interfere with the eggs, and the pea-hen herself was so cross that she would not allow anyone to approach her except the man who fed her. But such obstacles as these were nothing to me, and I had no difficulty in evading the watchers and abstracting the eggs from under the hen, without even disturbing her, or her being aware of the loss. Now here they are in my wallet, and when the loss is discovered presently, as it is sure to be, and a reward offered for their discovery, I propose to present them to the Emperor."

The other two Thieves applauded their comrade for his skill and ingenuity, and the second Thief then proceeded to relate his story as follows:

"When we separated yesterday, I at once entered the Emperor's antechamber, and mingled with the nobles and officials who were awaiting an audience with His Majesty, and amongst the others I soon noticed the Prime Minister. He was a very stout man, dressed in his finest robes, and with a new pair of boots on his feet. As he passed to and fro in the crowd, I succeeded in cutting the soles off his new boots without his having any idea of what had happened. Shortly afterwards he was summoned to the Emperor's presence, and when he knelt down to *kow-tow* before His Majesty, it was observed that he had no soles to his boots. The Emperor, thinking that the Minister had committed this serious breach of etiquette on purpose, fell into a violent passion, and ordered him to be imprisoned at once. It was no use for the wretched man to protest his innocence or to plead for mercy. The Emperor's orders are that, unless a satisfactory explanation is given to him before six o'clock this evening and the missing soles produced, the Minister is to be beheaded. Here are the soles of the Prime Minister's boots in my wallet, and I propose to present them to His Majesty this afternoon during his public audience. I shall thus earn the gratitude of the Prime Minister and appease the wrath of the Emperor."

The other two Thieves, on hearing this story, congratulated their comrade on his successful manœuvre, and the third Thief proceeded to relate his adventures as follows:

"When we parted yesterday," said he, "I entered the palace, and after wandering about for some time I found myself in the chamber where the Emperor's dinner was being prepared, and where all the chief officials of the palace were assembled to superintend the arrangements for the royal meal. There were the Head Chamberlain and the Under Chamberlains, the Head Usher and the Under Ushers, the Head Waiter and the Under Waiters, and many other officials of minor degree. I mingled with the servants, who were standing about, without attracting any attention, and remained in the room until the Emperor himself entered and seated himself with great ceremony to partake of his mid-day meal. The Chief Cook and the Chief Chamberlain placed themselves in front of the Emperor, in order to see that the service of his food was properly conducted, whilst the other high officials took their stand on either side of his chair and assisted in bringing in the dishes. In spite of all these precautions, however, I was able by my skill to take the food from each dish as it was placed upon the table, before the Emperor had time to partake of more than a very few mouthfuls. As the meal proceeded the Emperor grew more and more annoyed, and complained of the insufficiency of the food which had been prepared for him. Such a thing as this had never occurred before in the palace. The Head Cook and all the Under Cooks, the Head Chamberlain and all the Under Chamberlains, the Head Usher and all the Under Ushers, and all the officials of lower degree, were thrown into a dreadful state of confusion and alarm at the event. They rushed hither and thither, between the kitchens and dining-halls, upbraiding the scullions and other domestics for their carelessness, and preparing the most elaborate and copious dishes for the Emperor's table. But after some time the Emperor, wearied by the confusion, and unable, in spite of everything, to make a satisfactory meal, gave orders that the whole of the Cooks and other attendants responsible for his table-service should be imprisoned, and that unless a satisfactory explanation of their negligence could be given before this evening they should be beheaded. I have here, in my wallet, the whole of the viands which yesterday were placed before the Emperor for his consumption, and I propose at the audience to present them to him, and inform him what really happened. He will undoubtedly pardon me when he hears the story, and I shall earn the undying gratitude of all the disgraced officials by procuring their release."

The other two Thieves, on hearing this story, congratulated their comrade warmly upon his daring and success, and the three entered the Emperor's antechamber together, and awaited the time for public audience.

A few minutes later the great doors leading to the audience chamber were thrown open, and a herald appearing upon the threshold proclaimed "Silence." He then gave notice that, on the previous day, the eggs had all been stolen from under the Emperor's favourite pea-hen, and that any person who could find the eggs or give any information concerning their loss should receive a reward; secondly, that for a breach of etiquette the Prime Minister had been imprisoned, and that unless he could explain his offence before six o'clock that evening he was to be beheaded, and that any person who could offer assistance in the matter would be well paid and otherwise rewarded by the Emperor; thirdly, that owing to bad attendance during the Emperor's repast the previous day, all the domestic officials of the palace had been imprisoned, and would be beheaded at six o'clock that evening unless they could give a satisfactory explanation ; and that any person who could assist in the matter would be well rewarded for his pains.

So saying the Herald retired, and the public audience began. When the three Thieves were admitted to the Emperor's presence, they went in together and made a simultaneous obeisance before the Emperor's throne.

"Who are you three men ?" asked the Emperor, "and what do you want from me ?"

"May it please Your Majesty," replied the first Thief, "I have ventured to bring a small gift for you."

And so saying he took from his wallet the pea-hen's eggs, and laid them on the throne.

When the Emperor heard that these were his pea-hen's eggs he was very much pleased, and gave orders that they should at once be taken back to the nest, and the hatching continued ; and telling the first Thief to stand back, he enquired of the second what he wished to say.

"May it please Your Majesty," replied the second Thief, "I also have a small gift to make to you."

And so saying he took the soles of the Prime Minister's boots out of his wallet and laid them on the steps of the throne.

When the Emperor found that these were the soles of his Prime Minister's boots, and how they had been removed, he was very much amused, and laughed heartily. He at once sent orders for his Prime Minister to be released, and handed over to him the soles of his boots, and told him to watch them more carefully for the future. The Prime Minister was delighted at being reinstated in the royal favour, and expressed his gratitude to the Thief for his services in the matter.

When the third Thief was asked what he had to say he replied:

"I, too, have a small gift for Your Majesty."

And so saying he produced a plate from his wallet, and laid upon it the various viands which had been cooked for the Emperor's dinner the previous day.

When the Emperor understood that this was the dinner which had been prepared for him, and which he ought to have eaten, he was greatly astonished; but seeing that it was no fault of his Cooks, Chamberlains, or other servants, he ordered them all to be released, and to resume their former functions.

Having issued these various commands, the Emperor again summoned the three Thieves before him, and addressed them as follows:

"Although," said he, "I am very pleased at finding such a satisfactory explanation for the disappearance of the eggs, the misdemeanour of my Prime Minister, and the insufficiency of my dinner, I cannot overlook the fact that you three men have behaved in a very unusual manner. So before rewarding you in accordance with my promise, I desire to put your skill to a further test. If you succeed in this trial to my satisfaction you shall all three be well rewarded, and receive rank and lands in my country; but if you fail, you must take the consequences of your rashness, and you shall all three be put to death."

When the three Thieves heard these words they were greatly frightened, and bowing down before the Emperor they awaited his commands.

"The test which I have in store for you," continued the Emperor, "is as follows: you must know that in my Treasury I have a great number of jewels and precious objects of all kinds; and the Treasury is enclosed within a treble wall ten fathoms in height, closed by iron gates, and is guarded night and day by companies of my most faithful soldiers. If you can produce, before six o'clock to-morrow evening, three of the pearls from my Treasury, you shall be pardoned and rewarded; but if you fail to do so, you shall all three be put to death."

On hearing these words the three thieves consulted together for a few moments, and replied as follows:

"We will do our best to carry out Your Majesty's commands and to succeed in this test which you have given us, but we would call your royal attention to one matter; it is this: supposing we produce before to-morrow evening three pearls as you command, how shall we be able to satisfy you that they come from the Royal Treasury? All pearls look very much alike, and it would be impossible for us to prove to you whence they came. We would, therefore, venture to suggest that, before putting us to this test, you should have a complete enumeration made of all the jewels in your Treasury; then, when we produce the three pearls in question, it will be easy to ascertain whether there are in the Treasury three pearls less than there were when the enumeration was made."

The Emperor, seeing that this was a reasonable request, agreed to act as the Thieves had suggested. So summoning his Treasurer before him, he gave orders that a complete enumeration of all the jewels and other precious objects in his Treasury should be made before nightfall that evening; and having issued his commands he dismissed the audience.

The Chief Treasurer was much perturbed on receiving these orders, for owing to the enormous quantity of jewels and other objects in the Treasury, he foresaw that it would be a difficult matter to have the enumeration complete before evening. The only way in which it could be done was to call in the assistance of all the officials of the palace, and having allotted a section of the Treasure Chamber to each, to order them to make a complete inventory each of his own part. Accordingly, he called together all the officials of the palace to the number of many hundreds, and they proceeded in a body to the Royal Treasury. The three Thieves, who had anticipated this action on the part of the Treasurer, meanwhile dressed themselves up in the complete robes which are proper for a palace official, and mingling unnoticed in the crowd, they followed the Treasurer to the gates of the Royal Treasury. By the Treasurer's orders, the gates were at once thrown open, and the officials, entering the treasury, began the enumeration. The three thieves, in common with the rest, were allotted each a section of the Treasury Chamber, of which they were to make a complete inventory, and whilst so employed they had no difficulty in each one secreting a large pearl after first placing it upon their list. By nightfall the enumeration was complete, the lists were all handed over to the Chief Treasurer, and the Treasury was left locked and guarded as before.

Next day, at six o'clock, the Emperor seated himself in his Hall of Audience, and summoned the three Thieves before him.

"Well," said he, "have you been able to fulfil the conditions which I set you? If you can now produce three pearls from my Treasury, you shall be rewarded in accordance with my promise; but if you are unable to do so, you shall all three be put to death."

The Thieves bowed themselves humbly before the Emperor, and without making any reply each one produced a pearl and laid it on the steps of the throne. When the Emperor saw these pearls he was much astonished; but in order to make certain that they came from his own Treasury, he summoned his Chief Treasurer before him, and ordered him to compare the jewels in the Treasury with the inventory which had been made on the previous evening. The Treasurer hurried off to do so, and after a short while he reappeared, and informed the Emperor that, having carefully counted all the jewels, and having compared the numbers in the Treasury with the numbers on the inventory, he found that three pearls were indeed missing.

On hearing this the Emperor no longer hesitated

in fulfilling his promise to the three Thieves. He raised them at once to high rank, and presented them with lands and money sufficient to uphold their new status, and they lived happily ever afterwards, enjoying the confidence of the Emperor and the friendship of the numerous officials whom they had saved from imprisonment and death.

STORY No. XV.

THE STORY OF THE BOY WITH THE DEFORMED HEAD.

ONCE upon a time there lived a poor man and his wife who had only one child, and this Boy, as it happened, was born with a deformed head, which projected in front and behind, and gave him a very ugly appearance. The parents, although much grieved at their son's deformity, were, nevertheless, very fond of him and brought him up very carefully. Every day, when he grew big enough, he used to drive the cows out to pasture, and all day long he sat about on the hillsides watching the cattle graze. And so he passed his life very happily until, when he reached the age of fifteen, he began to think he should like to marry a wife as other young men did, but he feared that owing to his deformity no girl would ever look at him.

One day it chanced that he drove his cows to graze on the rich pasture on the edge of a small lake, and as he was sitting near the shore of the lake all of a sudden he saw a large white Drake descend from the sky, and light upon the surface of the water. As soon as it was seated upon the water it swam round the lake three times to the right and then three times to the left, and having done so it flew away again and disappeared into the sky.

The Boy watched the behaviour of this Drake with some interest. He had never before seen so large and beautiful a bird, nor one that behaved so strangely. So next day he again sat down in the same place, and kept a sharp look-out for the bird. At the same hour as on the previous day the Drake again appeared in the sky, and descending upon the lake, acted in precisely the same manner as before. And it continued to do so for several days, the Boy always watching its behaviour with increased interest.

At last he determined that he would try to catch this Drake for himself, so he wove himself a long rope of yaks' hair, big enough to completely encircle the lake, and he laid this upon the shore in a loop extending right round the lake; and at short intervals along the rope he fastened loops made of the finest horse hair, the loose ends of which he left floating in the water.

Next day the Drake came as usual and began to swim round the lake to the right. It had not gone very far when it put its foot into one of the loops and was caught. The Boy at once ran down to the shore of the lake, and taking the Drake in his hands, he tied its wings and legs together, and set it down on the grass beside him.

" Now," thought he to himself, " what shall I do with this fine white Drake ? I will take him home and kill him, and he will make a nice dinner for father and mother and me."

Just as he was thinking this, to his intense surprise, the Drake spoke to him as follows :

"I beg of you not to kill me, my good boy," said he, "for you must know I am not in reality a Drake as I appear to be, but I am a fairy King just come from the region of the gods. It is my habit every day to descend to this lake in the form of a white Drake, and to amuse myself by swimming round and round. If you will now consent to let me go I will reward you liberally. You shall have gold and silver and jewels and coral, as much as you wish, and sumptuous food every day for the rest of your life.

On hearing this the Boy laughed, and replied :

"You should not tell me such stories as these. How am I to know that you are really a fairy ? It seems to me that all you are in a position to give me is your feathers."

"I hope you will not disbelieve my word," replied the Drake very earnestly ; "I assure you I can do all this, and even more, if you will release me."

"Well," said the Boy, "if that is really so I will make a bargain with you. I do not care at all for your gold or your jewels, but what I really want is a wife. If you can promise to supply me with a wife I will let you go."

"Well," said the Drake, "that, too, can be arranged. I have three daughters living in my kingdom in the skies, and I will give you as wife any one of them whom you desire. Would you prefer the eldest, or the youngest, or the middle one ?"

The Boy was greatly pleased on hearing this offer of the Drake's, and he thought to himself:

"I will not take the eldest girl, for fear she should be too old, nor the youngest, for fear she should be too young. I will select the middle one."

So he told the Drake that he would like his middle daughter.

"Very well," said the Drake, "I will arrange the matter accordingly, and I will meet you here to-morrow with my middle daughter. But there is one condition which always attaches to the marriage of a mortal with a fairy, and that is that she can only live with you for nine years. At the conclusion of that time she is bound to return to her home in the heavens."

The Boy agreed to this condition, and when all the details had been satisfactorily arranged he cut the cords which bound the Drake and let him go. The bird spread his wings and flew up into the sky; and after circling for a few minutes he flew straight upwards and disappeared from sight, whilst the Boy went home to his father and mother.

The Drake flew far up into the blue sky until he arrived at the country of the gods, where he changed at once into the form and raiment of the King of the Fairies. Seating himself upon his throne, he summoned his three daughters before him and informed them of what had occurred; and he gave orders to his middle daughter to prepare herself forthwith to go and marry a mortal. The girl wept bitterly on hearing this, but nevertheless she prepared to carry out her father's orders, and got ready a large stock of beautiful clothes and much gold and silver and jewels to take with her.

Next day, at the appointed hour, the Boy went down to the lake as usual, and seated himself in his usual place; and not long afterwards he saw the white Drake and a white Duck flying towards him from the sky. They descended swiftly until they touched the ground, where they were at once transformed into the Fairy King and his beautiful daughter. The boy was overcome with joy when he saw the lovely wife that had been brought to him; but the girl was horrified at his ugly appearance, and begged her father to take her back to her abode in the skies. The Fairy King, however, insisted upon her carrying out her share of the bargain, so leaving his daughter with the Boy, he again turned himself into a Drake and, flying up into the sky, he disappeared from view.

The Boy now led his bride home to his father and mother, and next day the marriage was duly completed. The Fairy wife, by means of her magic, was able to erect a magnificent palace, and to furnish it in the most luxurious manner with everything necessary for comfort; and she supplied, moreover, horses and servants, and everything else that a married couple could desire. So the two took up their abode in this fine house and, together with the old father and mother, they lived there happily for several years; and as time passed away the fairy wife became accustomed to her husband's forbidding appearance, and year by year became more and more attached to him.

So the time slipped by and at last the nine years of the Fairy wife's abode upon earth came to an end. The young Man, however, had become so accustomed to her presence that he could hardly believe that the Fairy King's words would come true and that he should really be deprived of his wife when the appointed time arrived. So on the last night of the ninth year he went to bed as usual in his magnificent chamber, clothed in rich silks, and surrounded by all the evidences of wealth and luxury.

He slept soundly all night, and when he awoke in the morning and sat up and looked about him, what was his astonishment and horror to discover that, instead of lying upon his fine couch in his magnificent palace, with troops of servants ready to wait upon him, he was reposing upon the bare ground under the open sky, on a bleak hillside near to the spot where he had first conversed with the Fairy King. His palace, his servants, his horses, his furniture, and, worst of all, his beautiful wife, had all disappeared utterly and completely, and nothing remained of them but a memory. Half distracted with grief and chagrin, the young Man ran frantically across the country, thinking to find some trace of his lost happiness.

For some days he wandered on and on, scarcely conscious of what he was doing, and at length, having passed beyond the part of the country which he knew, he arrived one day about noon on the shores of a vast expanse of water which stretched before him as far as he could see. By the side of this lake there arose a jagged cliff, and about half-way up the cliff on a broad ledge he noticed an immense nest, in which appeared some young birds of unusual size. At first he was unable to detect what sort of birds these were, but after examining them attentively for some time he saw that they were three young Gryphons, whose parents apparently had gone off in search of food.

As he stood upon the beach watching the young birds they suddenly began to manifest every sign of terror and confusion, chattering and squealing wildly to one another, and flapping their puny wings; and on turning towards the lake in order to ascertain what was the cause of their alarm, he perceived an immense Dragon—whose head, at the end of its long neck, towered high above the water—making its way rapidly across the lake, with the evident intention of devouring the young Gryphons. The young Man, who was of a courageous and kindly disposition, determined to save the young Gryphons from the maw of this monster; so, drawing his sword, he waited till the Dragon had set foot upon dry land, and then, attacking him fiercely, he engaged single-handed in a desperate conflict. For some time the issue was doubtful, but the young man at length succeeded with one well-delivered blow in severing the Dragon's head from its neck, and the monster fell dead upon the beach.

Scarcely had the Dragon breathed its last when the air was darkened by the wings of some great creature passing overhead, and, looking up, he observed, flying just above him, the forms of the two parent Gryphons

THE DRAGON ATTACKING THE GRYPHON'S NEST.

now returning to their nest. As soon as they had arrived the young Gryphons proceeded to relate to them at full length the terrible danger they had just escaped, and the gallant conduct of the young Man in slaying their would-be destroyer. The parent Gryphons were very pleased when they heard this story, and, looking towards the young Man with some curiosity, they began to remark upon his appearance.

"Have you ever, Mother Gryphon," asked the male bird, "seen any creature of that description before?"

"No, Father Gryphon, I never have," she replied; "but it seems to be both brave and well-intentioned. I observe, moreover, that it has neither beak nor claws, so I propose that we invite it into the nest, and receive it hospitably in return for a good service which it has rendered to our children."

Father Gryphon agreed to this proposal, and he at once flew down to the beach, and addressing the young Man he invited him to enter the nest. The youth accepted the invitation, and having explained that he was unable to fly, he mounted upon the Gryphon's back and was speedily carried up the cliff, and deposited with the young Gryphons in the nest. After making a good dinner off the food which the parent Gryphons had just provided for their young ones, the young Man related to the family all his various adventures since the time when he had first made the acquaintance of the Fairy King.

"Yours," said Father Gryphon, "is a very sad story,

and in my opinion you have not been treated at all well; but if you desire it, I may perhaps be of some assistance to you. What I propose is that you should mount upon my back, and I will then carry you through the air to the kingdom of the gods, where you can represent your case to the King of the Fairies in person, and where you will, at any rate, have the opportunity of persuading your wife to accompany you back to earth."

The young Man gladly assented to this proposition, and mounted on the Gryphon's back; and the great bird, spreading his wings, soared upwards straight into the blue sky, carrying the youth with him. Up and up they flew, whilst the earth seemed to recede into the distance and to grow smaller and smaller, until at length it disappeared from view altogether. Still they flew on until, towards nightfall, they arrived at the country of the gods. The Gryphon, with the young Man upon his back, flew straight in through the great golden gates, and deposited the youth in the centre of a vast courtyard round which were sitting numbers of gods, fairies and other denizens of the sky.

When the gods saw that a human being had been deposited in their midst they rose in great wrath, and began bitterly to reproach the Gryphon for what he had done.

"How is it," said they, "that you have dared, unordered, to bring into our presence an inhabitant of the human world? Do you not know that human beings are of a coarser essence than ourselves and are repugnant and abhorrent to us? How dare you so defile the sacred country of the gods?"

But the Gryphon was not at all frightened at their anger, and he answered them boldly and firmly:

"This young man," said he, "is a valiant and kind-hearted youth. He saved my young ones from destruction by attacking, single-handed, and killing a Dragon who was on the point of devouring them. He then related to me his story of how, after nine years of happiness, he was deprived by the King of the Fairies of his wife, his house, his wealth, and everything which he had possessed. I consider, therefore, that he has been treated in a shameful and unjustifiable manner, and so I have brought him here to plead his cause in person and to claim redress."

While this conversation was in progress the young man's Fairy wife had been hiding in a corner, too nervous to show herself before her husband and all the assembly of the gods. But she could now contain herself no longer, and, rushing forward, she threw herself into her husband's arms, crying out that she loved him and would return with him to earth.

When her father heard this he did not know how to act, but it was decided that a conclave should be held, and the matter debated at length. So the celestial powers met together in a great council, and, having discussed the matter in all its bearings, they decided that, as the Fairy Princess desired to return to earth of her own free will, they would not stand in her way; but that if she did so, she must take the consequence of her own action, and that as the result of mating with an unclean creature like a human being she must herself become mortal and lose her Fairy nature.

On hearing this decision the girl joyfully agreed. So she and her husband mounted together upon the broad back of the Gryphon, and the great beast, spreading his wings, sailed through the golden gates of the palace and swept downwards through the blue heavens to the earth below. He soon deposited the youth and his wife on the ground near their old home, where he bade them farewell and returned to his own nest. And henceforward, although the Fairy had lost her magic powers, the two lived happily together, and grew to a good old age in prosperous and comfortable circumstances.

STORY No. XVI.

THE PRINCE AND THE OGRE'S CASTLE.

ONCE upon a time there lived an old King and Queen, who, although they had been married for many years, had no children to brighten their old age or to inherit their kingdom; and in the King's possession, as it happened, were a favourite mare and dog, who also had no offspring. Now both the King and the Queen were very anxious to have children of their own, and also to perpetuate the fine breed represented by the mare and the dog; so the King posted a notice all over his kingdom, offering a very large reward to any Lama or other holy personage who could secure to him and to his horse and dog the birth of children.

In response to this notice many Lamas and recluses presented themselves at the palace, and by means of prayers and religious ceremonies they endeavoured to obtain from the gods what the King and Queen desired; but all their efforts were in vain, and the years passed by without any offspring being born.

Now it chanced that in a neighbouring country there lived a terrible Ogre, who was an expert in magic and all the black arts; and it came to his ears that this King had offered a large reward if anyone could secure to him the birth of children for himself, his horse and his dog. So he disguised himself as a holy Lama; and coming up to the palace one day on foot, he asked for an interview with the King. The King, who had almost lost faith in Lamas of any kind, received him courteously, and asked him what he could do to help in the matter.

"Oh, King!" replied the supposed Lama, "I, you must know, am a great recluse, and as the result of many years of solitary meditation, I have become proficient in all the magic arts. I will undertake to secure for you and your horse and dog the birth of offspring as you desire. But I can only do so on one condition, which is as follows: three children will be born to you, three to the horse and three to the dog. They will all be of a miraculous nature, and will grow to their full powers in the course of three years. At the end of three years I will return here, and will claim from you one of each to follow me and serve me and to obey my orders in all matters."

The King gladly agreed to this condition, and asked the Lama how he should proceed in order to secure the desired result. The Lama replied:

"Here, oh King, are nine pills; three of these must be administered to the Queen, three to the horse and three to the dog. In three months' time a child will be born to each, to be followed by two others at intervals of one month."

So saying, he handed the pills to the King and forthwith took his departure. The King accordingly administered the pills as directed, and after three months the

Queen gave birth to a boy, the mare to a foal, and the dog to a pup, and these were followed by two others at intervals of one month as the Lama had predicted.

All the young ones grew apace, and at the end of the three years they had all attained to their full growth and powers, and punctually at the conclusion of the third year the Ogre, still disguised as a Lama, returned to the palace to demand his due.

The King and Queen, though reluctant to part with any of their children, resolved to abide by their bargain, and they consulted together as to which of the young Princes should be handed over to the Lama. After some consideration they decided that it would not be advisable to part with the eldest son, as he was heir to the throne, nor with the second, who would have to succeed to the kingdom should any accident or mischance befall his elder brother; so they resolved to send the youngest son, and with him the youngest horse and the youngest dog. These three accordingly were handed over to the Lama, who ordered the Prince to follow him, and started off at once to his own country.

After travelling for some considerable distance they arrived at the top of a high pass, whence the Ogre, pointing down to a great castle standing in the valley below, said to the young Prince:

"That is my house below there; I shall leave you here and you must go on down to the house. When you arrive there you will find a goat tied up near the door of the courtyard, and a bundle of straw lying near by. You must pick up the bundle of straw and place it within reach of the goat. Then you must go into the farmyard, where you will find many fowls, and in one corner you will see an earthenware jar full of soaked grain, and you must sprinkle this grain for the fowls to eat. These two tasks I give you to-day, and you are on no account to enter my castle until I rejoin you in the evening."

So saying the Ogre went off in another direction, whilst the young Prince, riding on his horse and followed by his dog, went down to the Ogre's castle. When he reached the gateway he found, as the Ogre had predicted, a goat tied up and a bundle of straw lying in a corner of the courtyard. So he dismounted from his horse, and, picking up the bundle, he carried it near the goat and placed it on the ground. Scarcely had the bundle touched the ground when it became transformed into three great wolves, who, leaping upon the goat, devoured it in an instant, and then fled away to the hills.

The young Prince was very much astonished at seeing this, but being of a courageous spirit he did not allow the incident to frighten him, and proceeded to finish the remainder of his task. So he entered the yard where the poultry were kept, and proceeding to the corner where stood the jar of soaked barley, he took out a handful and scattered it amongst the fowls. As the grain touched the ground it was transformed instantly into three wild cats, who leapt fiercely upon the cocks and hens, and in a few moments, having destroyed them all, fled away into the hills.

The Prince's curiosity was now thoroughly aroused, and he determined, in spite of the Ogre's warning, to enter the house itself, and to discover what sort of place he had come to, so he pushed open the door of the castle and began wandering about all over the house. For some time he found nothing to interest him. The rooms were all well furnished and in good order, but he could find no trace and hear no sound of any living creature.

At last, after having explored the greater part of the building, he suddenly turned a corner in a passage, and saw in front of him a room whose walls were composed entirely of glass. Entering this room he saw in one corner a beautiful lady lying asleep on a couch with a flower behind her ear. The Prince was pleased at finding a human being in this desolate and mysterious castle, and, approaching the lady, he endeavoured to arouse her from her slumber. But all his efforts were in vain; she appeared to be in a sort of trance, and all he could do did not succeed in waking her.

At last in despair he took away the flower which was placed behind her ear, and as he did so she woke and sat up upon her couch, rubbing her eyes. As soon as she perceived the young Prince she was much astonished, and asked him what he was doing in the Ogre's castle. The Prince told her the whole story of his miraculous birth through the magic of the holy Lama, and how he was condemned to serve the Lama as his servant through the agreement which the King his father had made, and how he had carried out the two tasks which the Lama had given him that day.

On hearing this story the lady was very indignant and spoke to him as follows:

"You must know, oh Prince," said she, "that the person whom you suppose to be a Lama is in reality a fearful and wicked Ogre. The only food of which he partakes is men's hearts, and this house is full of the lifeless bodies of his numerous victims. He, however, is unable to obtain any power over the body of a human being unless that being directly disobeys his orders. Thus it is his practice upon obtaining a fresh servant to set him strange tasks which terrify and repel him. These tasks grow daily more difficult and more odious, until at last one day the servant disobeys his orders, and forthwith his body is at the mercy of the Ogre, who devours the heart and places the lifeless body in a large chamber at the back of this house. The process has evidently begun with you to-day. You have fulfilled all of his tasks without allowing yourself to be terrified by the strange portents which you have observed, but on his return he will no doubt set you further and more disagreeable duties to perform. I, you should know, am a Princess in my own country, and I was handed over to the Ogre by my parents about a year ago in circumstances very similar to your own. But when he had brought me to his castle, instead of destroying me as he does his other victims, he fell in love with me, and I have remained here as his wife ever since. But he is of a very jealous disposition, and never allows me to leave his castle; and for fear I should make my escape during his absence, he invariably, before going out, places an enchanted flower behind my ear which makes me fall into a trance, and I cannot awake until the flower is removed."

The young Prince was very much interested on hearing this story, and he begged the Princess to give him some further information about the Ogre's habits, in order that he might not unawares fall into his power, and might eventually be able to bring about the destruction of the monster.

"It is very difficult," replied the Princess, "for any human being to kill the Ogre, for he is of a supernatural nature, and even if you were to cut off his head he would come to life again at once, unless you could also destroy his 'mascot'*—that is to say, the object upon the preservation of which his life in this world depends. Now the Ogre's mascot is very carefully concealed, and its existence and whereabouts are known to no person except myself. I, however, have discovered where it is, and I will reveal the secret to you later, but first I will tell you the method by which you may destroy the Ogre's body. You must know, then, that it is only possible for a human being to strike a mortal blow at the Ogre when his face is turned away. He knows this very well, and will never in any circumstances turn his back upon a man. Similarly, if he can make you turn your back to him he may be able to do you a mischief. When he comes in this evening and finds that you have fulfilled both the tasks he has set you, the first thing he will order you to do will be to walk three times round a great stove which stands in the centre of the kitchen; and if you

* Known as "La" in the Tibetan tongue. It is difficult to find an equivalent word in the English language, but the Princess describes its meaning. See also the story of "Koom Bacha and Baki," where the same superstition occurs.

obey his orders he will follow you from behind and will possibly do you some harm while your back is turned towards him. When he gives you these orders, then, you must not disobey, but you must tell the Ogre that it is so dark in the kitchen that you cannot see your way clearly, and you must ask him to precede you. This he is bound to do, and while he is going round the stove you may perhaps find an opportunity for stabbing him. If, however, you cannot succeed in doing so, and you both pass through this ordeal successfully, he will set you no further task to-night, and I will ascertain from him during the evening what trial he has in store for you to-morrow."

The Prince thanked the young lady for all her good advice, which he promised to follow faithfully in every respect, and she then said to him :

"It is now near the time for the Ogre's return. I will lie down on the couch, and you must place the flower behind my ear just as it was before; and when I fall into a trance you must at once go out into the courtyard and wait the return of the Ogre, and mind you are careful not to let him know that you have been inside the castle."

So saying, the Princess lay down upon her couch, and the young man having placed the flower behind her ear she instantly fell into a deep trance. The Prince then went out into the courtyard and shortly after the Ogre arrived. He had now discarded his lama costume and appeared in his proper form, and riding up to the Prince he asked him in an angry tone whether he had carried out the orders he had received, and on the Prince replying in the affirmative, the Ogre ordered him to come into the kitchen. On entering the kitchen the Ogre pointed to a great stove standing in the centre, and said to the Prince:

"You must now walk three times round that stove."

"It is so dark in here," replied the Prince, "that I cannot see my way at all clearly. Will you please precede me and show me the way?"

The Ogre was very angry at hearing this, but he was unable to refuse, so he started off and ran round the stove three times, the Prince following closely at his heels. But he went so fast that the Prince, although he had his knife ready in his hand, was unable to catch him; and the Ogre, seeing that the Prince was not to be outwitted by this stratagem, went upstairs to his wife, leaving the young man locked up in the kitchen, where he spent the night alone.

Next morning the Ogre started off soon after daylight on his own business, and as soon as he was gone the Prince ran upstairs to the glass room, where he found the lady lying in a trance as before. He took the flower from behind her ear, and she immediately woke up and looked about her.

"Good-morning, Prince," said she. "How did you succeed last night? I hope you followed the instructions which I gave you."

The Prince described to her what had occurred, and she said:

"I have ascertained what the Ogre proposes to dc

when he returns this evening. He will seat himself in his chair of state in his great hall of audience and will order you to *kow-tow* to him three times, and if you do so he will seize an opportunity whilst you are lying on your face before him to do you some injury. It will not do, however, absolutely to disobey his orders; but you must explain to him that, being a Prince, you have never had to *kow-tow* to anybody and do not exactly know how to do it, and you must ask him to show you the proper way to proceed. He cannot refuse your request, and you must take the opportunity of stabbing him or cutting off his head whilst he is lying on his face before you. If you succeed in this come at once to me, and I will show you what else is necessary in order to bring about his complete destruction."

The Prince promised to obey the lady's orders, and after again sending her into a trance by placing the magic flower behind her ear, he returned to the courtyard and awaited the Ogre's return. Just before dusk the Ogre came back and as the Princess had predicted he proceeded at once to the great audience hall, and seated himself on his chair of state.

"Now," said he to the Prince, "you must *kow-tow* to me three times."

"I am very sorry," answered the Prince, "that I do not know how to do so. Being a Prince myself, I have never had to *kow-tow* to anybody; but if you will show me the proper manner in which to proceed I will do my best."

This reply made the Ogre very angry, but he was

unable to refuse to do as the Prince had asked him. So the Prince took his seat on the Ogre's chair and the Ogre kneeling on the ground before him proceeded to *kow-tow* three times in the orthodox manner. As the Ogre's face touched the ground the first time the Prince drew his sword; as it touched the ground the second time he raised the sword above his head; and as it touched the ground the third and last time the Prince delivered a violent blow, completely severing the Ogre's head from his body. Leaving the body where it lay, the Prince ran up to the glass room as fast as he could, and having awakened the lady from her sleep, he told her what had happened.

"Well done!" said she. "The first part of your task is now accomplished; but as I told you before, it is still necessary to destroy the Ogre's mascot, or he will come to life again in a short time. What you must do now, therefore, is as follows: you must descend into the vaults below the castle, and having traversed nine dark subterranean chambers, you will come to a blank stone wall. You must rap three times on this wall with the hilt of your sword, exclaiming with each rap, 'Open, blank wall'; and as you pronounce these words for the third time the wall will fly asunder, and you will find yourself entering another subterranean chamber. In the centre of this chamber you will see a beautiful boy seated with a goblet of crystal liquid in his hand. This boy is the Ogre's mascot, and upon his existence depends the Ogre's life in this world. You must at once slay the boy, and taking the goblet very carefully in your hand, carry it upstairs to me. But be careful not to spill any of the liquid, as each drop means a man's life."

On receiving these instructions the Prince went down into the vaults at the basement of the castle, and having traversed nine great subterranean chambers, he found his progress stopped by a blank wall. Raising his sword he rapped three times with the hilt on the wall, exclaiming each time as he did so, "Open, blank wall." As he pronounced these words for the third time a grating sound was heard, and with a hollow clang the wall gave way for him.

Advancing a few paces the Prince found himself in a small dungeon, lighted only by the glimmer which issued from a goblet of crystal liquid held in the hand of a beautiful young boy, who was seated in the centre of the chamber. Without a moment's hesitation the Prince thrust his sword through the heart of the boy, and taking the goblet in his hand, he carried it upstairs to the Princess, being very careful on the way not to allow a single drop to be spilt.

When the Princess saw him entering her room with the goblet in his hand she was very much delighted.

"Now," said she, "the Ogre is effectually destroyed, and can never more come to life in this world. All that now remains to be done is to restore to life his previous victims."

So saying she ordered the Prince, still carrying the goblet, to follow her, and she proceeded by many winding passages and staircases to a remote part of the great castle. Presently, opening a huge door, she entered a long, low, gloomy chamber, lighted only by a narrow window which looked out over the back part of the castle. When the Prince entered this chamber he was horrified to see that down both sides of it were stretched the bodies of many scores of men, women and children, who lay there fully dressed, but to all appearance quite lifeless.

"These," said the lady, "are the bodies of the Ogre's victims; he has eaten their hearts, but the bodies, as you see, remain unharmed, while the spirit of each one is compressed into a drop of crystal liquor with which that goblet is filled. You must now sprinkle the bodies with the liquid, giving one drop to each."

Accordingly the Prince passed down the rows of lifeless bodies, dropping as he went one drop of the magic liquid on each body; and as the liquor touched the body the life returned, and each person, as if awakened from a long sleep, moved and yawned, and finally sat up and began to talk and walk. In a few moments the transformation was complete, and the Ogre's victims, after thanking the Prince and Princess heartily for their good offices, returned to their own homes. The Prince himself bade farewell to the lady, and leaving her in possession of the Ogre's castle and all its belongings, he himself mounted upon his horse, and with his dog following at his heels, set out in search of further adventures.

[This is only the first instalment of the Prince's adventures, which continue to an interminable length. I have given this section as a sample of the whole.]

STORY No. XVII.

THE STORY OF THE STONE LION.

ONCE upon a time there were two brothers whose father was dead, and who lived alone with their mother in a big house in a well-cultivated valley.

Now the elder of these brothers was a smart, clever man, but was of a very selfish, cold-hearted disposition; and the younger brother was simple and kind, but rather dull. The consequence was that after the death of their father the elder brother conducted most of the business of the family himself, and entirely supported his brother and his mother; whilst the younger brother, although quite willing to do his best, was not clever enough to be of any assistance in the household.

After a time the elder brother decided in his mind that he could no longer endure this state of affairs, so he one day called his young brother aside, and told him plainly that he would no longer continue to support such a lout, and that it would be better for him to go out into the world and seek his own fortune alone. The poor boy was much grieved on hearing this decision from his brother; but he was quite unable to protest or dispute, so, having packed up his few belongings, he went to say good-bye to his mother, and told her what had occurred. The good woman was very angry when she heard the news, and she said to her son :

"Very well, if your hard-hearted brother insists on turning you out of the house, I will accompany you. I cannot consent to remain any longer with such an unnatural and cruel son."

So next day the mother and her younger son left the house and set off together to seek some means of livelihood on their own account. After travelling for some little distance they reached an empty hut situated at the foot of a large hill, not far from a populous town ; and finding that the place was apparently deserted and that the owner, whoever he was, had left nothing to show that he proposed to return, they took possession of the hut, and slept there during the night.

Next morning early the boy, taking an axe with him, went out on to the hillside and began chopping wood. By evening he had chopped a fine big bundle of wood, and taking it down into the town he sold it in the market for a good sum of money. Greatly elated at the success of his labours he returned to his mother in the hut, and showing her the money he had earned, he told her that she need no longer have any anxiety regarding the future, for he would now be able to support her without any difficulty. Next morning, shouldering his axe, he started off again, and as before, began to chop wood. He had done a good morning's work, and was walking a little further up the hill in order to search for some better timber, when, in a sheltered part of the hillside he suddenly found himself face to face with a large life-sized Lion carved out of the stone.

"Now," thought he to himself, on seeing the Lion, "this, no doubt, is the guardian deity of this mountain, and to him must be due my good fortune in so easily obtaining a means of livelihood. I will certainly make him some offering to-morrow."

So that evening, after selling his wood, he purchased two candles in the town, and on the following day he went straight to where the stone Lion stood, and lighting the candles, he placed one upon each side of the image, and prostrating himself humbly upon the ground before it, he prayed for renewed good fortune. Suddenly, to his surprise and alarm, the Lion opened its mouth, and asked him what he was doing there.

The young man replied that having been driven from his home by his proud and hard-hearted brother, he was now engaged in earning his livelihood by chopping wood upon that hill; and that, thinking that the Lion must be the guardian deity of the mountain, he had considered it right to make him some sort of an offering, and to request his continued patronage and assistance.

"Very good," replied the Lion in a guttural tone of voice, "come again at this time to-morrow, and bring with you a large bucket, and I will furnish you at once with what wealth you require."

The boy thanked the Lion for his kindness, and carrying his load of firewood down to the village he sold it for a good price, and with the proceeds he purchased himself a large wooden bucket.

Next morning he went up onto the hill again, carrying his bucket, and arriving near the stone Lion, he again prostrated himself upon the ground and announced his presence.

"Very good," replied the Lion, "you must now act as follows: hold the bucket under my mouth, and I will vomit gold into it. But as soon as the bucket is nearly full you must tell me, as on no account must a single morsel of gold fall to the ground."

The young man proceeded to do as the Lion had instructed him. He held the bucket below the Lion's mouth, and the Lion forthwith began to vomit into it a stream of gold pieces. When the bucket was nearly full the young man informed the Lion of the fact, and forthwith the stream of gold came to an end; and the youth, having thanked the Lion most heartily for his munificent gift, carried off his bucket of gold in triumph to his mother. The poor woman was at first quite frightened at seeing so much wealth, but her son, having explained to her how he had come by it, she became greatly excited, and pleased.

Next day the widow and her son set about placing themselves in more comfortable circumstances. They purchased a large farm-house in the neighbourhood, and a large stock of cattle and sheep, and settled down in their new abode, and henceforward they began to live in a very comfortable and prosperous manner.

The news of the changed condition of life of his mother and younger brother soon reached the ears of the eldest son, and overcome with curiosity as to how this result had been brought about, he decided to call upon them, and to ascertain the cause of their prosperity. So, accompanied by his wife, and carrying with him a very small piece of cloth as a present, he set out to pay them a visit. When he reached the house his younger brother was away engaged upon his farm business, but the mother received her elder son and his wife very kindly and made them as comfortable as she could. In the evening, when the younger brother returned, he greeted his brother heartily, and being of a most kind-hearted and forgiving disposition, he related to him fully the manner in which he had come by his wealth, and strongly recommended his brother to act in a similar way.

The elder brother and his wife, as they returned home together that evening, talked the matter over between them, and decided that so good an opportunity of making money so easily was not to be lost. So next day the husband proceeded to the town, and after a prolonged search purchased the largest bucket which was to be had in the whole place. Carrying this with him, and bringing also a couple of candles, he proceeded to the hillside, and following the directions he had received from his brother, he soon found himself face to face with the stone Lion. He at once lighted his candles and placed them one on each side of the Lion, while he prostrated himself upon the ground, and prayed to the Lion for good fortune.

"Who are you?" said the Lion in a gruff voice; "and what do you want?"

"I," replied the elder brother, "am the brother of

THE STONE LION VOMITING GOLD.

Page 121.

the young man who was here the other day, and to whom you gave so much gold; and, following his advice, I have now come to ask you for a similar benefit for myself."

"Very well," said the Lion, "place your bucket under my mouth and I will vomit gold into it; but as soon as the bucket is nearly full you must inform me of the fact, as on no account must a single piece of gold fall to the ground. If this should happen, you will meet with misfortune."

So the elder brother, trembling with eagerness, held his bucket as directed, and forthwith a stream of gold pieces began to pour from the Lion's mouth into the bucket. The covetous fellow shook the bucket slightly from time to time in order to make the gold lie well together and so to obtain a larger quantity; and, overcome by greed, he could not bring himself to inform the Lion that the bucket was nearly full until it brimmed over and a piece of gold, slipping off the heap, fell to the ground. As it touched the ground the stream of gold suddenly ceased, and the Lion, in a hoarse voice, said:

"The largest piece of gold of all has stuck in my throat. Put your hand into my mouth and pull it out."

The elder brother, on hearing this, immediately thrust his hand into the Lion's mouth, hoping to secure a large lump of gold; and no sooner had he done so than the Lion, closing his jaws, held him fast. It was in vain that he struggled and wrenched his arm to and fro, endeavouring to release it; the stone jaws of the Lion gripped him so tight that he was totally unable to effect his escape, and the Lion, deaf to all prayers and entreaties, had relapsed apparently into an insensible figure of stone. And worst of all, when he glanced at his bucket of gold he saw, to his horror, that instead of gold it held nothing but stones and earth.

Towards evening the elder brother's wife grew anxious concerning her husband's absence, and knowing the direction in which he had gone, she set forth to the hillside to seek him. After hunting for some time she suddenly came across him, and asked him what he was doing and why he did not come home.

"Oh, wife," said he, "a terrible thing has happened to me. I put my hand into the Lion's mouth in order to extract a lump of gold which was stuck in his throat, when all of a sudden he closed his jaws, and gripped my arm, and now I am unable to effect my escape."

The poor woman, on hearing this, wept and wailed, but all her entreaties to the Lion proved of no avail, and she went off to her home, and soon returned carrying her husband some food. Every day, for many days after, she returned to her husband, bringing him such provisions as he required to keep him alive; but as she had now no one to work for her, and was obliged to support her husband and her child entirely by her own exertions, she became gradually poorer and poorer, and was soon obliged to sell her household goods to procure the necessary food.

Some months passed away and the poor woman,

falling ill, was at length reduced to such complete destitution that she had not even a morsel of bread to bring to her husband, and one morning she came weeping up the hill, and addressed him as follows:

"I have sold everything in the house, and have now no money to buy any food. There is not a scrap left to eat anywhere, and now nothing remains but for us to starve to death."

On hearing this the Lion was so tickled that he could not refrain from laughing.

"Ha, ha!" said he, and opened his great jaws.

As quickly as he could, and before the Lion had time to close his mouth again, the man withdrew his arm, and, finding himself free, he at once hastened down the hill with his wife. Then, taking their child with them, they proceeded straight to the house of the younger brother, and having related to him the whole of their story, begged some relief from their misery. The young man reproached his brother for his greedy conduct in trying to obtain an extra supply of gold from the Lion in spite of his warning; but being of a very forgiving nature, he consented at last to supply his brother with a sum of money sufficient for him to take a small farm in the neighbourhood. Here the proud brother and his wife settled down in very humble circumstances, whilst the younger son lived for many years very happily with his mother and prospered exceedingly in all he undertook.

STORY No: XVIII.

THE STORY OF THE LAMA'S SERVANT.

THERE was once an old Lama who lived in a small house at the very top of a hill in a lonely part of Tibet. He was a very holy man and spent his time entirely in religious contemplation, and the only person whom he allowed about his house was a certain young man of low birth, who acted as his Servant and used to cook his meals and perform other household duties. This man was a great character in his way. He was an amusing fellow and very fond of his joke, but was quite unreliable and incapable of performing any regular work.

Now the old Lama's diet, in accordance with the tenets of his religion, was a very small one, and he refrained entirely from taking the life of any living creature. So his food consisted chiefly of barley-flour, butter, and so on, and he abstained from meat of any kind. This mode of life, however, was not at all pleasing to the Servant, Rin-dzin, who had a healthy appetite and greatly missed his daily dish of meat, and he was constantly trying to persuade the Lama to allow him to kill a sheep or a goat in order that he might have a satisfactory meal. This, however, the Lama always sternly refused to do, and forbade his Servant on any account to destroy the life of a living being.

One day the Servant noticed a fine fat sheep, which, having become separated from the rest of the flock, was wandering about near the Lama's house. So he pursued it and caught it, and carrying it into the ground floor of the house, he went up into the room above, and letting down a rope through a hole in the floor he hitched a slip-knot at the other end of the rope round the sheep's neck. Having made these arrangements he went into the next room, where the Lama, as usual, was sitting alone wrapt in religious contemplation, deaf to all mundane affairs.

"Oh! Lama," said the Servant, addressing the old man, "I have come to tell you that I have just found a sheep belonging to our neighbours, who live in the valley below, wandering about near the house; so, for fear he should be eaten by wolves, I have caught him and tied him up in a room below. But he is a very violent sheep and is struggling desperately to escape. Will you be so kind as to hold the rope for a short time while I go and inform the owner where his sheep is?"

The old Lama, who never refused a reasonable request, at once proceeded to do as he was asked, and, rising from his seat, he followed the Servant into the next room.

"Pray hold this rope," said the Servant, handing the Lama the loose end of the rope to which the sheep was secured, "and if the sheep begins to struggle, pull it as hard as you can to prevent him from escaping."

The Lama accordingly took hold of the rope, and the Servant went down into the lower storey as if he intended to leave the house. Instead of doing so, however, he went into the room where the sheep was tied and began to poke the animal with a sharp stick, and the sheep began to struggle violently, trying to escape from its tormentor. The more the sheep struggled below the more the Lama pulled above, and at last, when the tug-of-war had lasted for some minutes, the sheep was strangled by the slip-knot round its neck.

After the lapse of an hour or two the Servant returned to the Lama in the upper room and informed him that the sheep had died a natural death while he had been away seeking for its owner, and, in the circumstances, he supposed that they might as well cut it up and cook it for food. The unsuspecting old Lama agreed to this, and for several days the Servant was able to eat his fill of excellent mutton.

It chanced, however, that the shepherd boy who was in charge of the sheep had come to the Lama's house looking for the one which was lost, and peeping in through the window had seen all that had happened. He told the story to his parents, who were very angry, and came to complain to the Lama of the conduct of his Servant. The old Lama was very much incensed at the treachery and wickedness of his attendant, and dismissed him on the spot, telling him to go away and never come back again. So Master Rin-dzin, with his few belongings on his back, marched off into the world to try and make his fortune.

He was a good deal cast down at first, but being naturally a volatile, light-hearted fellow he soon recovered his spirits and marched along the road singing blithely, and keeping a sharp look-out for anything that might turn up. He had not proceeded very far when he fell in with another young man going in the same direction as himself, and the two, joining company, fell into conversation. Rin-dzin soon related to his young friend all his recent adventures, and informed him that he was anxious to make a little money.

"Very good, brother," replied the Stranger, "I am the very man to help you, for you must know I am a thief by profession, and I am always on the look-out for what fortune may bring me. So we will join company, and it will indeed be bad luck if we cannot succeed in hitting upon something profitable before many days have passed."

So they went along together and towards evening they came upon a large house standing in a fertile valley. The Thief went forward alone to make enquiries, and he soon returned to Rin-dzin with the information he had gathered. The servants of the house had told him that the owner had died the day before, and was now awaiting burial in his own room. His only relation was his daughter, who was heiress to the whole of the property, and she was now mourning for her father all alone in the big house. Further, the Thief had learned that the old man had once had a son, who had run away from home many years before and had never been heard of again.

"Now," said he to Rin-dzin, "I have a plan to propose to you. Do you climb in through the window into the room where the old man's body lies awaiting burial, and conceal yourself somewhere. As soon as you are ready I will go to the young lady of the house and inform her that I am her brother, who has returned home after many years' wandering. She will probably disbelieve my story, and I will propose that we should consult the corpse of her father on the matter. When we come into the room where the corpse lies I will address it, and ask whether I am not the long-lost son, whereupon you must reply that I am. On this evidence I shall secure at least one-half of the property, which, of course, I shall share with you. But be careful on no account to leave the room before morning, otherwise you are sure to be detected by the dogs which roam about the house by night."

Rin-dzin agreed to this proposition, and climbed in by the window into the dead man's room, and, concealing himself near the corpse, he awaited the arrival of his friend. Meanwhile the Thief went boldly up to the front door and gave a loud knock; and being admitted by the servants, he went straight to the chamber of the young lady of the house.

"Who are you?" said she; "and what do you want?"

"Oh! sister," he replied, "I am your long-lost brother; do you not recognise me?"

"No," said she, "it would be impossible for me to recognise you, as I was only a little child when you ran away. No one but my father could know you and he, alas! died yesterday."

"That is very sad," replied the Thief, "for indeed it will be difficult for me to prove the truth of my story. Let us, however, go into the room where my father's corpse is lying, and ask it whether or no I am his long-lost son."

The girl agreed to this, and the two went together into the chamber where the old man's corpse was sitting trussed-up for burial, in accordance with the Tibetan custom.

"Are you there, father," said the Thief, as he entered the darkened room; and Rin-dzin, in a sepulchral voice replied, "Ah."

"I have come to ask you," went on the Thief, "whether or no I am your long-lost son."

"You are," replied Rin-dzin.

And on hearing this the Thief at once retired, followed by the young girl, who was now completely convinced of his identity.

"Now, sister," said the Thief, addressing her when they were alone together, "you see that my story is true, but, unfortunately, I am unable to stay here as I am called away this very night on urgent business. I will therefore make over to you the house and the whole of the landed property, and all I ask from you as my share of the estate is a bag of gold, as big as I can carry with me."

The girl accepted these conditions, and handed over to the Thief a heavy bag of gold. He then bade her farewell and started off with his booty as fast as he could, leaving Rin-dzin behind him in the same room as the corpse.

Early next morning Rin-dzin climbed down from the window, and coming round to the front of the house he asked the lady where her brother was.

"Oh!" said she, "I gave him a big bag of gold last night, and he at once started off with it as fast as he could."

When Rin-dzin heard this he was very angry indeed at the Thief's treachery, and was determined to follow and punish him. So, borrowing a horse from the lady of the house, he galloped off down the road as fast as he could. About mid-day, as he was galloping along, he saw the Thief some distance ahead, sitting under the shade of a tree resting; for not knowing that Rin-dzin had a horse, he did not consider it necessary to go very fast.

When Rin-dzin caught sight of the Thief, he first thought that he would at once go up to him and demand his share of the gold, but on second thoughts he remembered that while he himself was unarmed, the thief possessed both a sword and a musket, so that if it came to a quarrel between them he would probably get the worst of it. So, leaning down over his horse's neck, he pretended not to see the Thief, and galloped past him down the road, as if in mad pursuit. As soon as he was out of sight of the place where the Thief was sitting he pulled his horse up to a wall, and taking a new boot out of the bundle on his back, he dropped it in the middle of the road, and then pursued his way for some little distance further, when he took the fellow boot out of his bundle and dropped it also in the middle of the road. Having done this he turned aside from the roadway and concealed himself and his horse in a thicket near by.

As soon as Rin-dzin had galloped out of sight, the Thief congratulated himself at not having been seen, took up his bag of gold and continued his journey. After walking some little way, he came upon a new boot lying in the centre of the road.

"Ah!" thought he, "that foolish fellow has dropped one of his boots in his haste. But one boot isn't worth picking up; it is of no use at all. What a pity it is he did not drop them both."

So leaving the boot where it lay, he resumed his journey. The sun was now very hot, and the Thief, carrying his heavy bag of gold, was getting pretty tired, and by the time he reached the place where the other boot was lying he was nearly worn out.

"Hallo," said he to himself, when he caught sight of the second boot, "here is the other boot. This is really too good a chance to be lost; I must certainly go back at once and pick up the first boot, and then I shall have a pair of new boots for nothing. But I can't carry this heavy bag of gold all the way back with me."

So thinking, he concealed the bag of gold under a

tuft of grass by the roadside, and started off to retrace his steps to pick up the first boot. No sooner was he out of sight than Rin-dzin emerged from his hiding-place, and picking up the bag of gold, strapped it to his saddle and rode on his way.

STORY No. XIX.

THE COUNTRY OF THE MICE.

ONCE upon a time there was a King who ruled over a large tract of country in which there lived a great number of Mice. Generally the Mice were very prosperous and had plenty to eat, but it happened one year that the crops of the country were very poor, and the Mice, who subsisted chiefly on the spare grains left after the harvest, found that their stores were running short before the end of the winter. So the King of the Mice decided that he would make a petition to the King of the country, to lend the Mice what grain they required on condition that they repaid the whole amount the following year.

So he dressed himself up in his best clothes and set off one morning to the King's palace. When he got to the door of the palace the door-keeper asked him where he was going.

"Oh!" replied the Mouse, "I wish to see the King of the country, as I have a petition to make to him."

When the King heard that a Mouse wanted to see him he was very much amused, and he ordered that the little animal should be admitted.

When the Mouse entered the King's presence he

walked slowly up the Hall of Audience, carrying in his hand a little silk thread, which he presented to the King, instead of the usual ceremonial scarf.*

"Good-morning, Brother Mouse," said the King, "what can I do for you?"

"Oh! King," replied the Mouse, "you must know that this year our crops have fallen short, and we are threatened with a famine unless we can borrow sufficient grain to carry us through the winter; so I, who am King of the Mice, have come here to ask you if you can help us in this matter. If you can lend us the grain we require, we will repay you faithfully with interest at the next harvest."

"Well," said the King, "how much grain do you want?"

"I think that we shall require," said the Mouse, "one of your big barns full."

"But," said the King, "if I were to give you a barn full of grain how would you carry it away?"

"Leave it to me," said the Mouse; "if you will give us the grain we will undertake to carry it off."

So the King agreed to present the Mice with one of his great granaries full of barley, and he ordered his officers to throw open the doors, and to let the Mice carry away as much as they wanted.

That night the King of the Mice summoned all his subjects together, and to the number of many hundreds of thousands they invaded the barn, and each one picked

* This is in accordance with Tibetan custom, whereby a scarf is invariably presented upon all occasions of ceremony.

THE CROW AND THE FROG IN THE GUTTER

up as much grain as he could carry in his mouth, on his back, and curled up in his tail, and when they had all finished the barn was empty, and not a single grain of barley was left.

Next morning, when the King went out to look at his barn, he was very much astonished to find that the Mice had been able to empty it so effectually, and he conceived a very high opinion of their powers; and when, in the following spring, the King of the Mice redeemed his promise by repaying with interest the loan he had taken from the King of the country, the latter saw that they were trustworthy as well as clever.

Now it happened shortly after this that the King of the country went to war with a neighbouring kingdom, which lay on the opposite side of the river forming the frontier between the two countries. This other country was far more wealthy and powerful than the country where the Mice lived, and its King soon assembled a huge army on the opposite bank of the river and began making preparations for invasion.

When the Mice heard what was happening, they were much distressed, for they feared that if the enemy entered their country and destroyed their friend the King, they themselves would suffer considerable hardships under a strange ruler; so the King of the Mice set out again to visit the King of the country, and when he reached the palace he demanded an interview with His Majesty. This was at once accorded to him, and finding the King looking very depressed, he addressed him as follows:

"I have come to you a second time, Oh King, in order to see whether I can be of any use to you. The last time I was here you did me and my people a great favour, for which we shall ever be grateful, and if it is now in our power to assist you in any way, we shall be very glad to do our best."

The King, in spite of his grief, was much amused on hearing these words from the Mouse.

"Why," said he, "what could the Mice do to help me in my present predicament? We are threatened with invasion by a foreign army, outnumbering mine by many thousands, and all the men I can muster will not be sufficient to enable me to repel the enemy. I don't see how the Mice can help me."

"Do you remember, Oh King!" replied the Mouse, "that on the last occasion I was here you doubted our ability to carry away the grain you had given us, or to repay you the loan? And yet we proved ourselves able to do both. All we ask you now is to trust us again, and if you will undertake to do one or two things which we ask of you, we on our part will undertake to rid you of the invading army."

The King was a good deal struck by this remark of the Mouse, and he replied:

"Very well, what you say is quite true; and if you will inform me what you wish me to do, I will undertake to carry out my share of the bargain."

"Well, then," answered the Mouse, "all we wish you to do is to provide us by to-morrow evening with one

THE MICE CROSSING THE STREAM.

hundred thousand sticks, each about a foot long,* and to have them laid in rows on the bank of the river. If you will undertake to do this, we on our side will undertake to stave off the threatened invasion and to put the opposing army into a state of confusion and panic. And if we succeed in carrying out all we promise, we will ask you for the future to safeguard us against the two principal dangers which threaten the existence of the Mice who live in your country."

"I will gladly do what I can," replied the King, "to safeguard you against these dangers if you will tell me how to proceed."

"The two dangers to which I refer," continued the Mouse, "are flood and Cats. You see the majority of our burrows are in the low-lying land near the river, and whenever the river rises a little it overflows this level country and floods our nests. What we would suggest to you is that you should build a strong dam all down the river bank so as to ensure that the water cannot overflow into our nests. And as to the Cats they are always the persecutors of Mice, and we ask you to banish them altogether from your kingdom."

"Very well," replied the King, "if you can succeed in averting the danger which now threatens us, I will undertake to do all that you ask of me in this respect."

On hearing this, the King of the Mice salaamed profoundly to the King, and returned as fast as he could to his own subjects.

On the following evening he marshalled all the full-grown Mice of his kingdom, and about dusk, he led down a large army numbering several hundreds of thousands to the edge of the river, where he found the sticks all laid out as had been arranged with the King. In accordance with instructions they had received, the Mice at once proceeded to launch these sticks on the river, and they themselves embarked upon them two or three at a time; and so, pushing off from the bank, they sailed across the river and soon landed on the opposite side.

It was now quite dark, and the enemy's soldiers were all asleep in their camp, some lying in tents and some in the open air, with their arms beside them ready for any alarm. The Mice on a word of command from their King, scattered themselves without delay through the sleeping camp, and each one began to do as much destruction as he possibly could in the shortest possible space of time. Some nibbled at the bowstrings and the slings of the soldiers' muskets; others gnawed the slow-match and fuses; whilst others bit off the clothes and pigtails of the sleeping men. In fact, they attacked fiercely anything upon which their teeth could make an impression, and tents, stores, grain, and provisions of all kinds were soon reduced to shreds or scattered in confusion in every direction; and after a couple of hours' work they all collected upon the river bank, and, embarking again on their sticks, they sailed quietly over to their own shore without having been detected by the enemy, or even having caused any alarm.

STORY No. XX.

THE STORY OF THE TORTOISE AND THE MONKEY.

THERE was once an old Tortoise who lived with his wife and family in a large lake, on the borders of which grew an extensive jungle; and in the forest there were many wild beasts, more especially Monkeys, who swarmed in great numbers all along the shores of the lake.

It happened one day that the Tortoise came out of the lake and went for a stroll amongst the trees which grew near the water. After walking for some distance he became hungry, and looking up into a cocoanut-tree, near which he found himself, he thought how much he should like to get one of the cocoanuts which were growing near the top. He made several awkward attempts to climb the tree, but the stem was so straight and so smooth that he was quite unable to succeed; and he was just about to give up the attempt in despair when he espied a large Monkey sitting among the branches. The Monkey, who had been watching the Tortoise's attempts to climb the tree with some curiosity, felt rather sorry at his failure, and noticing that the Tortoise was a fine, well-grown fellow with a very handsome shell, he thought he would do him a kindness, so breaking off one or two of the cocoanuts, he threw them down to the Tortoise, who gratefully ate the fruit.

The two animals now entered into conversation with one another, and soon striking up quite a friendship, the Monkey led away the Tortoise into the jungle, and showed him a comfortable cave where he could spend the night. The Tortoise was so interested with all he saw and so pleased with his friend the Monkey, that he remained for several days in the forest, moving about during the day and sleeping with the Monkey in the cave every night.

Meanwhile Mrs. Tortoise was becoming rather anxious concerning her husband's prolonged absence. He had never been away from home for so long before, so finally she despatched one of the young Tortoises to find out where his father was and how he was getting on. The young Tortoise accordingly swam to land, and after hunting about for some time in the forest he came across his father near the cave.

"Good-morning, Father," said he, "Mother has sent me to find out where you are and how you are getting on."

"Oh, I am all right, my boy," replied Father Tortoise; "tell Mother she need not trouble about me. My friend, Brother Monkey, and I are just having a good time in the forest, and I will be home in a few days. Now run off to your Mother."

So the young Tortoise went back to his mother and told her what had happened. Mrs. Tortoise was not at all pleased at her husband's conduct.

"It is quite time," thought she, "that he should return to his wife and family, instead of amusing himself with a vulgar Monkey in the forest."

So she sent the boy back again to his father, with a message to say that Mrs. Tortoise was very ill, and that her physician had told her that the only thing to cure her was a Monkey's heart. So he must return at once to his home and bring a Monkey along with him.

The young Tortoise accordingly proceeded to hunt out his father again, and as soon as he met him he gave him Mrs. Tortoise's message. On hearing the news of his wife's illness, Mr. Tortoise became much alarmed, and reproached himself for having stayed away for so long; and in order to secure the necessary medicine for his wife he informed his friend the Monkey that he was obliged to return home at once on urgent business, and he invited the Monkey to come and spend a few days at his house. The Monkey accepted his friend's invitation, and the two set off together to the shores of the lake.

When the Monkey understood that it would be necessary for him to enter the lake, he became rather alarmed, and remarked to the Tortoise that never having been in the water, he was afraid it would be difficult for him to reach the Tortoise's home.

"Never fear about that, Brother Monkey," said the Tortoise; "I can arrange that quite simply. If you will mount upon my back, I will swim with you wherever we want to go."

So the Monkey mounted upon the Tortoise's back, and the Tortoise set out to swim to his house.

As they went across the lake the Tortoise began telling the Monkey about his wife's illness, and in doing so he foolishly let out that the only medicine to cure her was a Monkey's heart. On hearing this the Monkey became very much alarmed, and saw that he was being led into a trap.

"Dear me, Brother Tortoise," said he, "I am very much grieved to hear of your wife's illness, but if she is as bad as all that I do not think that one Monkey's heart will be enough. I should think that three or four at least would be required in order to effect a cure. If you like, I can easily get several other Monkeys from amongst my friends to accompany us to your home."

The Tortoise thought that this was a good idea, and agreed to carry the Monkey back to the shore and await him there while he went off to fetch some other Monkeys. So he turned round and swam back through the lake till he reached the edge, where he waddled out on to the beach.

As soon as he found himself on dry land the Monkey skipped off the Tortoise's back as fast as he could, and climbed to the top of the tallest tree he could find in a twinkling. On reaching the top of the tree he began reviling the Tortoise, and calling out every bad name he could think of.

"You are a nice sort of friend," said he, "to ask me to pay a visit to your home in order to kill me and use my heart as medicine for your ugly wife. Do you call that a proper return for all my attention to you, and for showing you all over the jungle? However, I have

THE MONKEY CALLING INTO THE TORTOISE'S CAVE.

been too clever for you this time, and you will have to do without my heart for many a long day to come. And as to the hearts of those other Monkeys that I promised to you—well, you can just wait till you find them for yourself."*

The Tortoise, on hearing these words, fell into a violent passion, and made several efforts to climb the tree in order to punish the Monkey, but being quite unable to climb at all, he soon gave up his attempt and determined to get even with the Monkey in some other way. So he hid himself in the water until evening, and as soon as it was dusk he came out on the land and proceeded very quietly to the cave where he and the Monkey had lived together, and concealed himself in the darkest corner of it waiting till the Monkey should come in.

The Monkey, however, was a good deal too clever to be caught in a simple trap like this. When his usual bedtime arrived, he came to the mouth of the cave and looking in, he called out in a loud voice:

"Oh, great cave! great cave!"

The Tortoise lay low in his dark corner and gave no sign of life.

After a few moments' silence the Monkey again called out:

"Oh, great cave! great cave!"

Still the Tortoise lay low and gave no sign.

"Curious thing," said the Monkey to himself in an audible tone of voice, "very curious! There used always to be an echo in this cave, but I can't hear the slightest echo to-night. There must be something wrong," and saying this he again called out :

"Oh, great cave! great cave!"

The foolish Tortoise, thinking that if he simulated an echo the Monkey would enter the cave as usual, hereupon gave answer from his dark corner:

"Oh, great cave! great cave!"

On hearing this the Monkey chuckled to himself at the simplicity of the Tortoise, and went off to sleep in some other part of the forest.

THE GLASS PILLARS DANCING FOR THE OGRE.

STORY No. XXI.

THE STORY OF ROOM BACHA AND BAKI.

ONCE upon a time, in the country of Room, there lived a King called Bacha, who, having married a young Princess from a neighbouring kingdom, lived with her for a short time very happily. But it happened that both the King and Queen were of a very argumentative turn of mind, and were constantly disputing with one another about all sorts of trifles, and as neither would ever give way to the other, it generally ended in their quarrelling. The King, who was a proud and headstrong man, was not at all pleased that his wife should venture to maintain her opinion against his, and gradually became very much incensed against her.

One night, as the two were sitting together after dinner, a fox began to bark in the palace grounds outside.

"Ah!" said the King, "do you hear that tiger roaring?"

"My dear," replied the Queen, "that is not a tiger, it is a fox."

"Certainly not!" said the King. "Do you think I don't know a tiger when I hear him? There can be no question but that it is a tiger."

The Queen again contradicted him, and a heated argument ensued, in which neither convinced the other. At length, the King said that he could not stand this argument any longer, but would submit the question for decision to his council on the following day. If the council agreed that he was in the wrong, he should be sent adrift on a log of wood on the great river that flowed past the palace; but if the Queen should be found to be in the wrong, she should suffer this fate.

So next day the King summoned a council, composed of all his wisest ministers and men of science. When they were all seated in the council chamber, he addressed them as follows:

"Last night," said he, "some beast began to bark outside the palace. I maintained that it was a tiger; the Queen affirmed that it was a fox. I desire to submit the question to you for decision. If you decide that it was a fox, I agree to be sent adrift upon a log of wood on the great river which flows past my palace; but if you think that the animal was a tiger, then the Queen is to suffer this penalty."

So saying, the King withdrew, leaving his ministers to decide the question. The counsellors, after weighing the matter for some time, summoned to their presence several peasants living in the neighbourhood, and these being all agreed that no tiger ever came within many miles of the palace, whereas foxes prowled there nightly, it was clear to the council that the King was in the wrong. Before any decision was given, however, the oldest counsellor rose and addressed the meeting as follows:

"It appears to me," said he, "that the King is undoubtedly in the wrong in this matter; but I wish to point out to you that if we announce our decision to that effect, the consequence will be that we shall be left without our King, and with only a Queen to reign over us. This, as you know, is a most undesirable state of affairs. I propose, therefore, that in spite of our real opinion in the matter we should make a public announcement to the effect that the King was right in his argument."

The others agreed to these words of wisdom, and the counsellors proceeded in a body to the King's throne-room and informed him publicly that after due deliberation they had come to the conclusion that he was undoubtedly in the right. The King was greatly pleased at hearing his opinion confirmed, and at once gave orders that the Queen should be sent adrift on the river astride a log of wood. So the poor Queen was taken down to the river bank, and placing herself astride of a log of wood, she floated off down the great river.

After floating along for several hours the current at length carried her to the opposite bank, many miles away from her own country, and as soon as she arrived in shallow water she waded ashore and looked about her. As far as she could see, the whole country appeared to be one great plain, covered with high grass, through which it was almost impossible for anyone to force their way; but after hunting about for a time, she discerned a small opening in the grass, which led her to a narrow winding path, along which she walked for some considerable distance. After going some way she came suddenly upon an open clearing in the grass, in the middle of which a very old man, with a white beard reaching almost to his waist, was seated before a small fire cooking himself some food.

"Good-morning, sir," said the Queen, when she saw him; "can you give me a morsel of food, for I am very hungry."

"Certainly, Madam," replied the old man; "you are welcome to all I have," and so saying, he handed over to her the whole of his provisions.

When the Queen had made a good meal, the old man addressed her as follows:

"You must know," said he, "that I am a magician, living in this prairie, and you must carefully follow the directions which I shall now give you. You must first follow the path, which will lead you to the top of a small hill, and when you arrive there a son will be born to you. This boy is not an ordinary human child, but is the incarnation of a very holy Lama, with miraculous qualities, and he will from his birth be able to walk and talk. His name is Baki, and you must follow him wherever he leads."

The Queen thanked the old man for his advice, and following the narrow path, it soon led her to the top of a small hill; and here she was delivered of a child, who, as the magician had predicted, was of a miraculous nature, and was at once able to walk and talk. The boy without any hesitation went forward along the path, followed by his mother, and after travelling for some distance they emerged from the great grass jungle into an open cultivated country.

Now it happened that on that day the three sons of the King of that country were out hunting together, and as they rode along looking out for game they suddenly came upon the Queen and her son. Having heard her story, they mounted her and the boy upon a horse and carried them off to the King's palace. The King at once took them under his protection, and gave orders that the boy should be brought up with his own sons, and he and his mother lodged in apartments in the palace.

Baki grew rapidly in beauty and stature, and soon became an expert in all sports and games. One day he and the King's three sons were out hunting together, when by chance they suddenly came upon a beautiful snow-white doe, who jumped up before them and galloped off towards the mountains. The four young men at once started off in pursuit; but the horses upon which the King's sons were riding gradually tired, and one after another they dropped out of the hunt, leaving Baki to continue alone. As the chase continued the poor doe began to show signs of exhaustion, and Baki, who was close upon her heels, was feeling confident that he would soon catch her. All at once the deer galloped straight up to what appeared to be a precipitous rock, and touching the rock with her muzzle, it flew asunder, revealing the entrance to a great cave within; and as she crossed the threshold of the cave her skin fell from her, and she appeared in the form of a beautiful young woman. Baki, who was of a very courageous disposition, did not hesitate for a moment, but, leaping from his horse, he followed the lady into the cave, and scarcely had he entered when the rock doors closed behind him with a loud crash. Following the form of the lady along a narrow passage, he emerged presently into a great lofty apartment, hollowed out in the centre of the rock, luxuriously furnished and brilliantly lighted, and with a row of great glass pillars running down the centre.

The girl meanwhile had seated herself upon a couch in one corner of the room, and addressing the young man, she asked him who he was, and what he meant by thus thrusting himself upon the privacy of a lady. The young Prince apologised, and explained the circumstances of the case as best he could, whereupon the girl addressed him as follows:

"You must know," said she, "that the place where you now find yourself is the abode of a terrible and bloodthirsty Ogre, and that I, who am human like yourself, was captured by him some time ago, and he proposes shortly to make me his wife. Meanwhile he has taught me certain magic spells, which enable me to transform myself into any animal I please, and to come and go at my pleasure; but without the assistance of some human being it is impossible for me to escape from his clutches. But we will talk further regarding these matters tomorrow. It is now near the time for the Ogre's return, and if he finds you here he will certainly kill you without the least hesitation, so you must hide now before he returns."

So saying she went over to the central glass pillar

and, unscrewing a portion of it, she showed him a cavity inside, within which he concealed himself.

Scarcely was he securely hidden within the pillar when the door of the cave flew open, and a huge Ogre entered the central chamber. Calling the young lady to him, he commanded her to bring his dinner, and after making a sumptuous repast he sat down on some cushions and began playing the guitar. At the first sound of the music all the pillars in the room, with the exception of the one in which Baki was concealed, began a slow and stately dance, his pillar alone remaining firm and unshaken. When the Ogre saw that one of the pillars was not dancing as usual he grew very angry, and seizing a huge hammer in his hand, he advanced upon it, threatening to shatter it into a thousand fragments; but the young lady, seizing him by the arm, begged him to spare it.

"Look," said she "at the position of the pillar. It is the most central and the largest of them all. No doubt it feels some sense of dignity and wishes to be distinguished from the remainder. Spare it at any rate to-night, and it will probably dance as usual to-morrow."

The Ogre agreed to this, and shortly after retired to rest.

Next morning at daybreak he set off about his business, and as soon as he was gone the girl opened the pillar and released Baki, and after giving him a good breakfast, she spoke to him as follows:

"It is a very difficult thing," said she, "for a human being to kill an Ogre, for whatever damage you may do to his body is of no avail unless you can also destroy the object with which his spirit is bound up. Now this particular Ogre's existence depends upon the life of a green Parrot, which is carefully hidden from human view, but I have ascertained where it is kept, and will explain to you how you may find it. Behind the rock in which we are now living you will find another great rock standing by itself. You must go up to this, and, kicking it three times with your right foot, you must exclaim at each kick, 'Great Raven, open the door.' As you pronounce these words for the third time the door will open, disclosing a large cave, in the centre of which, seated upon a red stone, you will see a green Parrot. If you can kill this Parrot you will also destroy the Ogre without any danger to yourself."

On hearing this Baki at once promised to follow the lady's directions, and she released him from the cavern. Going round to the back of the rock, he found himself face to face with another great rock standing by itself. Kicking this rock three times with his right foot, he pronounced the magic words, and as he said them for the third time two rocky doors flew open, disclosing a cave inside. Entering the cave he saw a green Parrot seated on a red stone in the centre, and he at once seized the bird and wrung its neck. As soon as he had accomplished this he ran hastily back to the main cavern, and as he approached the entrance he saw the Ogre, who had just been returning to his home, lying across the threshold stone dead, with his neck all twisted. The young lady was greatly rejoiced at the successful issue of their adventure, and the two, leaving the Ogre's body behind them, proceeded forthwith to the capital of the country, where the King's palace was situated.

On arriving at the capital Baki decided to hire a small house, where he could lodge the young lady and change his own dress before proceeding to pay his respects to the King; so having taken a house in the suburbs, he left the lady there while he went out himself into the streets to hear the news. He soon found out that during his absence the King had announced his intention of marrying Baki's mother, and the poor lady, now that she had no son to protect her, had protested in vain, saying that she was already the wife of another. Baki was very indignant when he heard of this treacherous conduct on the part of the King, and determined to foil his plans. So returning to the young lady, he related to her all that he had heard.

"Do not be anxious," said she. "If you will follow my advice I will show you how you may yet get the better of the King,"

And she forthwith instructed him in certain magic spells, which she had learned from the Ogre.

Armed with these, Baki proceeded at once to the palace. When he arrived in the courtyard he sat himself down upon the King's mounting-block, and muttering the necessary spell, he was at once transformed into a large cowrie-shell. After lying on the mounting-block for some time it chanced that one of the grooms of the palace passed by, and, seeing the shell, he paused to look at it, and remarked to himself:

"What a beautiful cowrie-shell!"

"Yes, I am a very handsome shell," replied the cowrie, to the terror and astonishment of the groom.

"Why," said he, "what sort of a shell are you? What can you know about cowries, or anything else?"

"I know a great deal," said the shell. "For instance, I could tell the King something about Prince Baki, which perhaps he would not like to hear."

When the groom heard this he ran straight into the palace and informed the Prime Minister all that the shell had said. The Minister, having told the King of the matter, the King gave orders that the shell should at once be brought into his presence and placed upon a table before him. When this had been done the King addressed the shell, saying:

"What are you, and what do you know about Prince Baki?"

"I can tell you this," replied the shell, "that if you attempt to marry Prince Baki's mother you will find yourself in a very unpleasant position."

On hearing this the King was very much incensed, and he ordered one of his servants to bring in a big hammer to smash the shell to fragments, saying that he would not be browbeaten by a wretched little object like a shell. So one of the servants, bringing up a hammer, struck the shell a violent blow and broke it to pieces. In an instant each piece of the shell turned into an armed man, and Prince Baki himself appeared amongst them in his proper form.

Great confusion now arose amongst the courtiers;

some fled in one direction and some in another, whilst others, drawing their swords, prepared to fight with the strangers. Meanwhile the armed men, who were in reality demons, placed temporarily under the command of Prince Baki, looked fiercely around them, and waving their swords, shouted to the Prince, "Whom shall we kill? Whom shall we kill?"

Baki now pointed to the King, and in a moment the band of armed men fell upon him, cut him to pieces, and disappeared with shouts of triumph through the roof of the palace. When the courtiers saw what had happened, they hastened to prostrate themselves before the feet of so powerful a magician, and installed Baki as their new king.

As soon as he was seated upon his throne he sent for the young lady whom he had rescued from the Ogre's cave, and, having married her, they lived happily for many years. And the Queen, his mother, soon after returned to King Bacha, and having agreed with him never more to argue on trivial matters, they had no more disputes or quarrels, and long reigned together over a contented and prosperous kingdom.

STORY No. XXII.

THE STORY OF THE HOME-BRED BOY.

HOW HE FOUND THE LOST TURQUOISE.

THERE was once an old woman living in Tibet whose husband had died and left her alone with her only son.

As the Boy grew up, his Mother grew more and more fond of him, and disliked parting from him even for a moment. She was afraid that if he left her house and began wandering about by himself some accident might happen to him, and she would be left desolate in her old age. So the older he grew the more careful she became, until at last she saw that it was impossible to restrain the Boy any longer, and it would be necessary for him to go out into the world to seek his fortune, just as other young men of his age had to do. So when he had reached the age of fifteen she waited till the fifteenth day of the sixth month, which is a very auspicious date, and calling the Boy to her, she presented him with a new suit of clothes, a horse, a dog, a gun and a sword; and she told him that he was now at liberty to leave his home and to go out into the world to seek his fortune.

The Boy was greatly delighted at receiving these gifts and with the prospect of meeting with some adventures, so after saying farewell to his Mother, he mounted his horse, and with the dog trotting at his heels he started away down the road. All day he rode quietly along by himself without meeting with any adventures, and towards evening he reached a high plateau near the top of a range of mountains. As he was crossing the plateau a fox jumped up in front of him and ran off towards the mountains. The dog, on seeing the fox, started to chase it; while the young Man, thinking he was to have some fun at last, galloped after the dog as fast as he could.

After running for some distance the fox suddenly disappeared into his earth, and the Boy, riding up, dismounted at the mouth of the hole, and began to scheme how he was to catch the fox when he came out. So he took off his cloak* and fastened it to the saddle with his sword and his gun, and then placed his horse a little to one side of the fox's earth, whilst his dog stood ready at the other side; and he himself took off his hat and put it over the mouth of the hole, and taking a large stone in his hand, he crouched down ready to slay the fox when it came out.

After sitting waiting for some time the fox all of a sudden darted out of its earth, and ran off towards the hills, with the Boy's hat sticking over its head. It came so suddenly that he had no time to hit

* In Tibetan "chu-ba," the outer garment, like a dressing-gown, worn by all Tibetans.

it with his stone, or to interrupt its flight. The dog, on seeing the fox go off, at once started in full pursuit; and the horse, excited by the dog's cries, galloped off after the pair, and in a few moments all three were lost to sight in the gathering darkness. The poor Boy found himself in a moment bereft of all his possessions—his horse, his dog, his gun, his sword, his hat, and even his outer robe, which he had strapped on his saddle, had all disappeared. After running after his horse for some distance he gave it up in despair, and lay down to pass the night as best he could under a big poplar tree.

He woke towards dawn, and, looking up into the branches of the tree, he saw a large Raven's nest, on which an old Raven was sitting hatching her eggs, whilst Father Raven perched on a branch near by. When day broke the two Ravens began talking to one another.

"Good-morning, Father Raven," said the old bird on the nest, "who is this sleeping under our tree?"

"That," replied Father Raven, "is a foolish home-bred Boy who has no experience of the world. In trying to catch a fox last night he lost his horse, his gun, his sword, his dog, and even his clothes, and now he has not the least idea where to find them."

"Yes, so I see," replied Mother Raven, "but it is clear, nevertheless, that all he has to do is to go towards the villages which lie towards the east from here—there he will meet with good fortune."

On hearing this the Boy at once started off towards the east, and proceeding for some little distance, he met an old Beggar Man, to whom he related the whole of his story, and asked him if by any chance he had seen the missing property. The old Man, seeing before him only a poor Boy, without even a hat or a cloak, did not believe a word of this story, so he only laughed at him and mocked him; and finally, when the Boy grew angry, gave him a sound beating, and left him to go on his way disconsolate.

Wandering on a little further, he came to a big house where a wedding feast was being celebrated. Coming timidly up to the door of the house, he peeped in at the guests, and presently one of the servants happening to pass by, he related his sad story. But just then the Bridegroom caught sight of him, and called out in a rough voice:

"Who are you who come crying here at my wedding feast? We want no woebegone faces here to-day to bring us bad luck. Go away, you ill-omened creature."

So the poor Boy slank away sadly, and after wandering about till nightfall he reached another large house further towards the east. After the reception he had received from the wedding party he was afraid to go in or to knock at the door, so creeping into the backyard he dug himself a nest in the manure heap, and crouched down in this for warmth, all hidden except his head. Thus he spent the night comfortably enough.

Early next morning the pigs belonging to the place began to poke about the yard and the manure heap, and several of them, as they passed, rooted at his head with their snouts to see if he was anything good to eat.

He could not stand this very long, so finally, screwing up his courage, he went to the back door of the house, and asked one of the servants to lend him a knife, saying that he wanted it to cut up the dry meat which formed his breakfast. The servant lent him a knife, and as soon as he had got it he enticed one of the pigs away to a quiet corner, where he killed it and cut off its head; and taking with him some strips of its flesh, he returned to his nest in the manure, and hid himself there again, together with the pig's head, waiting to see what would turn up.

Towards noon the Lady of the house came out into the yard, and as she was moving about superintending the various farming operations, it happened that a large and valuable turquoise fell out of her headdress without her noticing it. When, after a few minutes, she went back into the house, leaving the turquoise lying in the middle of the yard, the Boy thought that this would be a good opportunity of getting the turquoise for himself, but he was afraid to leave his nest for fear of being noticed; so picking up a piece of rag from amongst the manure he threw it over the turquoise, concealing it from sight.

Shortly after, one of the maid-servants came out of the house, and seeing a piece of rag lying in the middle of the yard, she picked it up, and the turquoise with it, and thrust them both into a crevice in the wall.

Just then a great uproar arose from the house, where the Lady had discovered the loss of her turquoise. The whole household was summoned, and set to work to search for the missing jewel. For some time great bustle prevailed, everyone searching hither and thither, and ransacking every hole and corner; but no one thought of examining the piece of dirty rag thrust carelessly into a crevice of the farmyard wall.

Finding that all their efforts were of no avail, the Lady of the house sent off in hot haste to summon all the most famous diviners, magicians, and lamas of the neighbourhood, and these, when they arrived, began practising all kinds of spells and casting auguries in the hope of discovering what had become of the turquoise; but all in vain, and when nightfall arrived, they were no better off than they were before.

Towards evening they packed up their various magical instruments and spells, and went away very downhearted; and as soon as they were gone the Boy emerged from his hiding-place, and going boldly to the house, he said that he was a famous magician and could find the turquoise for them; and he asked that on the following morning all the diviners and lamas should again be summoned, as well as the inhabitants of all the neighbouring houses. The Lady of the house was at first inclined to ridicule the idea of this disreputable-looking beggar being able to accomplish what none of these famous sorcerers could do; but thinking it worth while to give the Boy a chance, she decided to do what he suggested, and meanwhile ordered her servants to let him have a good supper, of which he stood badly in need.

Next morning, about ten o'clock, a large crowd of people assembled in the courtyard of the house. In addition to the magicians and lamas of the day before, a great many of the neighbours had obeyed the summons, and amongst them were the people who had treated the poor Boy so badly during their wedding feast, and the Beggar who had reviled and beaten him. As soon as they were all seated in rows ready to see what was going to happen, the Boy, holding the pig's head under his arm, presented himself before them all, and addressed them as follows:

"Now," said he, "I hope in a few minutes to be able to discover the missing turquoise, for I am possessed of magic qualities of unusual power. In my search I shall be assisted by this enchanted pig's head which I hold under my arm. Owing to the spell I have cast upon it, it is able at once to detect a thief or a dishonest person, and also to discover stolen property."

So saying he took the pig's head in both hands, and holding its snout towards the company, he went round from person to person, halting for a moment in front of each. Presently he arrived in front of the Bridegroom, who had been so rude to him some days before, and the pig's head at once became violently agitated, and kept poking itself towards this man.

"Ah!" said the Boy, "here is evidently a dishonest man; it is no good our proceeding any further in our search until he has been beaten and turned out of here."

The other people at once seized upon the wretched man,

One of the Story-tellers, with his Family and Servants.

and after giving him a severe thrashing, they turned him out of the place. Next to him was sitting the Beggar who had so insulted the Boy, and who had disbelieved his story. Here, again, the pig's head became violently agitated, and the Beggar, too, was well beaten and turned out. Having got rid of these two persons, the Boy now began to walk round the yard, the pig's snout apparently sniffing carefully at every part of the wall in the farm buildings. Presently, coming to the crevice into which the rag had been thrust by the servant-maid, he moved the pig's head violently to and fro.

"Ah!" cried he, "the missing turquoise must be somewhere near here."

On hearing this everyone began to search about in that neighbourhood, and in a few minutes the turquoise was found inside the rag thrust into the crevice of the wall.

The Mistress of the house on recovering her turquoise was greatly elated. She took the Boy into the house, and having presented him with a new suit of clothes, and given him all he wanted to eat and drink, she handed him a large sum of money, and he went on his way in a far better plight than when he had first arrived there.

THE HOME-BRED BOY.

HOW HE DISLODGED THE SPIDER.

AFTER leaving the house where he had found the turquoise, the home-bred Boy wandered along until, towards nightfall, he arrived at the same poplar-tree where he had previously stayed the night, and, lying down under its branches, he fell fast asleep, and did not wake up until towards morning.

As day was dawning the two Ravens overhead began talking to one another as before, and the boy overheard their conversation.

"Good-morning, Father Raven," said the hen bird on the nest. "What kept you so late last night?"

"Well," replied Father Raven, "the fact is, I was visiting a farmhouse down yonder, where the mistress of the house, as it happens, is very ill. She is suffering from a severe pain in her left ear, which drives her almost distracted, and no one about the place knows what it is nor how to cure it. They have consulted all of the most famous doctors and lamas in the neighbourhood without, however, affording her any relief at all. Indeed, no one knows what is the cause of the disease except myself. I have ascertained that the pain in her ear is due to the fact that some days ago a large Spider effected an entrance during her sleep, and that the Spider and her young ones have now taken up their abode inside the Lady's head. It is impossible to dislodge them except by a stratagem. As you are aware, Spiders are in the habit of sleeping all through the winter months, and only wake up and emerge from their retreat in the spring. If it were possible to make the Spiders believe that spring had arrived, they would come out of the ear at once; otherwise they will remain there all through the winter."

"Indeed," replied Mother Raven, "that is very interesting; but how would it be possible to make the Spider believe that spring had come?"

"There is a very simple stratagem, which I have often seen employed," replied Father Raven, "which is as follows: a piece of green cloth must first be spread upon a table and well sprinkled with water, and the Lady must bend her ear over this so that the Spiders can see it. It will appear to them to be a green field, wet with the spring rains, and they will imagine it is time to come out; and then, if they still display any reluctance to emerge, it is only necessary to beat a drum to simulate thunder. Thunderstorms, as you know, only occur in the spring, and the Spiders on hearing this noise will feel convinced that spring has really come, and will emerge without any further hesitation. The moment they come out on the table they must be wrapped up in the cloth with the greatest expedition and carried away and killed, for if this is not done, they will always be ready at the slightest alarm to climb back into the ear by the threads which they have left suspended behind them."

Mother Raven thanked Father Raven for his information, and she then said:

"But you yourself are not looking at all well this morning, what is the matter with you?"

"Well," said he, "I am sorry to say I over-ate myself yesterday. The people of the house kept praying to the gods, and were all day long occupied in making offerings of rice and flour. Most of these offerings were thrown out into the garden, and I was able to eat as much as I wanted. In fact, I ate a great deal too much, and I fear that I am going to die. If I do, you must faithfully promise to remain in mourning for me, in accordance with Tibetan custom, for three years, three months and three days."

Mother Raven, on hearing this, was greatly affected, and solemnly vowed to carry out the wishes of her husband, and poor old Father Raven, getting into the nest, shortly after breathed his last.

As soon as he was dead Mother Raven remarked to herself that she had a great deal too much to do in looking after her family and household duties to think for a moment of following so absurd a custom as mourning for a dead bird for any period at all. So she pushed old Father Raven's body out of the nest with her bill and let it fall to the ground below, while she herself flew off to find food for the young ravens, which had just been hatched out.

Meanwhile the Boy, who had listened attentively to the colloquy of the Ravens overhead, went straight off to hunt for the house where the Lady was suffering from pains in her ear, and he decided in his own mind to make this another opportunity for displaying his magical powers. He soon arrived at the house in question, and found the whole family in great grief, and the poor mistress of the house suffering torments with the pain in her ear. Going to the house he asked what was the matter, and on hearing the cause of their sorrow he at once announced that he was possessed of very wonderful magic powers, and was prepared to effect a cure. The people of the house who had seen him on the previous day, when he had found the turquoise, were inclined to believe him, and asked him what they should do to procure relief for their mistress.

"All that is necessary," replied he, "is a square piece of green cloth, some clean water in a jug and a couple of drums."

When these things had been made ready he spread the piece of green cloth on the table and sprinkled some water over it, and he then told the Lady of the house to lean across the table so that her painful ear should come above the patch of green cloth. No sooner had she done so than the Spiders inside, seeing the green expanse with water still lying upon it, thought that the spring had come and began moving about, and the old Mother Spider at once let herself down by a thread to see if it was really spring.

The people of the house were greatly astonished at

seeing the Spider emerge, but the Boy ordered them not to touch her; and having satisfied herself that there was really water on the cloth, she climbed again up her thread, and went back into the Lady's ear to impart the good news to her family. The Boy now ordered the drums to be beaten, and on hearing this sound the whole of the spider family, thinking that the noise was thunder, and that spring had undoubtedly arrived, hastily emerged from the Lady's ear and let themselves down, one after another, on to the green cloth. As soon as they were all, to the number of seven, arrived upon the table, the Boy snatched up the piece of cloth, and wrapping up the spiders inside it, he carried them all outside and destroyed them.

The Lady of the house was now completely cured and overwhelmed the Boy with gifts and compliments, and he left the house carrying with him a large sum of gold, in addition to that which he had received the day before. He now bent his steps towards his Mother's house, and as he was going along the road to his home he suddenly came face to face with the old Beggar who had previously insulted him, and whom he had had beaten and turned out when he was looking for the turquoise. The old man, who was of a very jealous and vindictive temper, was very much incensed against the Boy, and had determined to avenge himself upon him. As the Boy came down the road the old Beggar suddenly emerged from behind a clump of bushes, holding a sword in his right hand and a fly in the hollow of his left fist.

"Now," said he, "I believe you to be an impostor. You have twice made pretence to magical powers, which in reality you do not possess, and I am about to put you to a final test. If you can tell me what I hold in my left hand I shall let you go free; but if you fail to do so, I shall immediately kill you with this sword."

The poor Boy was greatly alarmed at hearing these words, and having no weapon himself he was completely at the old man's mercy. So at a loss to know what to say, he replied:

"Well, then, you can kill me if you like, for I am as much in your power as though I were a fly which you hold in your left hand and which you can crush at your pleasure."

The old man was so much astonished at hearing this reply, which he looked upon as a proof of the Boy's supernatural powers, that he forthwith became one of his most ardent admirers; and as he had seen where the Boy's horse, dog, and other belongings had disappeared to on the occasion when they had all followed the fox, he was able to lead the boy to a distant valley, where he found his horse and dog together. Here having recovered his sword and his gun, his clothing and other possessions, he mounted upon his horse and followed by his dog he returned to his Mother's house a very much richer Boy than when he had left it.

THE HOME-BRED BOY.

HOW HE DEFEATED THE ENEMY.

On his return to his home the home-bred Boy found that he was now famous far and wide for his supposed magical powers, and he was constantly consulted by people of all classes, who wanted his assistance in their various affairs.

It happened not long afterwards that a war broke out with a neighbouring country, and the King sent for the Boy, and asked him whether he would be able to give any assistance in the campaign against the enemy. The Boy was rather alarmed at this request of the King's, for he did not in the least know how he should set about defeating the foe, but he allowed no sign of hesitation to appear in his manner, and he answered boldly that he was prepared to undertake the job; whereupon the King presented him with a magnificent charger and begged him to do his best.

Now as it happened, the Boy was in reality a very bad rider, and did not at all fancy the idea of riding about on a spirited horse, but for very shame he could not refuse the King's gift. So early next morning, when he mounted his horse with the intention of riding out and reconnoitring the enemy's camp, in order to see what could be done, he made his servant tie his feet together with a rope under the horse's belly, so that he should not fall off if it ran away or played any pranks with him. Having ridden for some distance he reached the top of a hill, whence he could obtain a clear view of the enemy's camp, and as he was sitting on his horse watching the scene below a trumpet suddenly sounded. The noise of the trumpet frightened the horse, which, after giving one or two preliminary plunges, dashed off down the hill at full gallop straight towards the enemy's camp.

The poor Boy was much terrified at this untoward event, and did all he could to stop his horse by pulling the bridle and speaking to it, but with no avail. Just before reaching the camp the horse carried him under a dead tree, and the Boy, raising his arms, seized one of the branches with both hands in the hope of checking the horse's mad career; but the rotten bough broke in his grasp, and the horse continued its gallop right into the camp, with the Boy holding in his hands a huge branch of the tree.

Hither and thither rushed the horse amongst the tents of the enemy, trampling the frightened soldiers underfoot, whilst the Boy in his struggles to maintain his balance, swept his great branch to and fro with equally disastrous effect. During his gallop his hair had become loosened, and was now flying wildly in the air, and his shouts and adjurations to his horse increased the terror of his appearance. The enemy's soldiers had never seen such a terrific-looking object before, and one and all came to the conclusion that he must undoubtedly be a demon that was attacking them, and that he would soon compass their entire destruction. So instead of opposing him they tried to soothe and conciliate him, offering him silken scarfs and other presents as he galloped to and fro. But he made no reply to them, and continued to shout fiercely at his horse.

These shouts were taken by the soldiers to be threats of vengeance against themselves,* and, finally, the General and all the principal officers, coming out in a body with scarfs, begged him to make peace and to allow them to go away quietly. The Boy, who heard what they said, was quite willing to agree, but was totally unable to control his horse, so he shouted to them that he accepted their submission on condition that they were able to stop his horse. So running on either side of him, they seized the bridle and soon brought the animal to a standstill, when the Boy formally accepted their surrender, and dictated to them terms of peace; and they on their part were only too thankful to have escaped from such a danger, and gladly consented to withdraw at once to their own country.

When the King heard what had happened, he sent for the Boy and thanked him very heartily for his services; and as a reward for what he had done, he raised him to the highest rank, and presented him with lands and gold, and the young Man and his Mother lived happily ever afterwards.

* There is a play on the words of the Tibetan original here which explains this point, but which is incapable of adequate translation into English.

SOME VERSES FROM TIBETAN LOVE-SONGS.

A woman sings to a man whose affection for her is waning :

" As a great mountain, with its cooling streams,
Nourishes the little fields far down below,
Do you, my lover, with a stream of love,
Nourish the heart of her who loves you so."

The man replies to the woman :

" When autumn chills destroy the honeyed flowers,
The bees must do without their favourite food ;
So when my passion cools, and dies my love,
You should submit to this my changéd mood."

A man sings to a woman :

" Up every rocky cliff some path exists,
If one can find a guide to show the way ;
So to your heart some avenue must lead,
Teach me, forthwith, that path of love, I pray."

The woman replies :

" Were I inclined to grant this fruit* to you,
The gift were thine at once—to-day, to-morrow.
But oh ! I fear that lurking at your back,
Are demons red† to bring me endless sorrow."

* *I.e.*, her heart. She compares her heart ripe with love to a ripe fruit.

† Presumably she means the man's passions. She compares them to the terrific demons (red is the angry colour) of Tibetan Lamaist mythology.

LOVE SONG.

Could I but win the maiden
  For whom my heart doth pine,
I'd prize her as a jewel
  From depths of ocean brine.

I'd guard her fragrant body,
  Like white turquoise so rare.
My wanderings all behind me,
  I'd know no earthly care.

As luscious fruit well ripened,
  Hangs tempting on the tree;
So is thy beauty, maiden,
  Temptation sore to me.

From longing for thy beauty,
  How can I sleep at night?
By day I seek thee vainly,
  My heart is tired quite.